Bamboo Cage

D1253285

The New Brunswick Military Heritage Series, Volume 13

◾ Bamboo Cage

THE P.O.W. DIARY OF FLIGHT LIEUTENANT ROBERT WYSE, 1942-1943

Edited by Jonathan F. Vance

GOOSE LANE EDITIONS and
THE NEW BRUNSWICK MILITARY HERITAGE PROJECT

Copyright © 2009 by Jonathan F. Vance.

All rights reserved. No part of this work may be reproduced or used in any form or by any means, electronic or mechanical, including photocopying, recording, or any retrieval system, without the prior written permission of the publisher or a licence from the Canadian Copyright Licensing Agency (Access Copyright). To contact Access Copyright, visit www.accesscopyright.ca or call 1-800-893-5777.

Edited by Brent Wilson and Barry Norris.
Front cover illustration by Australian War Memorial (ART26492). Murray Griffin. Interior view of 100-metre hut, Changi, 1944, brush and brown ink and wash over pencil, 37.4 x 53.6 cm. Australian War Memorial (ART26492).
Back cover illustration: Typical prison camp (albeit a very tidy one), as drawn by Dutch prisoner Andrew van Dijk. Collection of Jan Krancher.
Cover and interior page design by Julie Scriver.
Printed in Canada on paper containing100% post-consumer fiber.
10 9 8 7 6 5 4 3 2 1

Library and Archives Canada Cataloguing in Publication

Wyse, Robert, 1900-1967.
    Bamboo cage: the POW diary of Flight Lieutenant Robert Wyse, 1942-1943 / Robert Wyse; Jonathan F. Vance, editor.

(New Brunswick military heritage series: 13)
Co-published by: New Brunswick Military Heritage Project.
Includes bibliographical references and index.
ISBN 978-0-86492-529-9

1. Wyse, Robert, 1900-1967.   2. World War, 1939-1945 — Personal narratives, Canadian.
3. World War, 1939-1945 — Prisoners and prisons, Japanese.   4. Prisoners of war — Indonesia — Java — Biography.   5. Prisoners of war — Canada — Biography.   6. Great Britain. Royal Air Force — Biography.
I. Vance, Jonathan F. (Jonathan Franklin William), 1963-   II. New Brunswick Military Heritage Project   III. Title.   IV. Series.
D811.W97 2009   940.54'7252092   C2008-907179-4

Goose Lane Editions acknowledges the financial support of the Canada Council for the Arts, the Government of Canada through the Book Publishing Industry Development Program (BPIDP), and the New Brunswick Department of Wellness, Culture and Sport for its publishing activities.

Goose Lane Editions
Suite 330, 500 Beaverbrook Court
Fredericton, New Brunswick
CANADA E3B 5X4
www.gooselane.com

New Brunswick Military Heritage Project
The Brigadier Milton F. Gregg, VC,
Centre for the Study of War and Society
University of New Brunswick
PO Box 4400
Fredericton, New Brunswick
CANADA E3B 5A3
www.unb.ca/nbmhp

To Robert N. Wyse,
and to his grandson, Robert J. Doucet,
whose desire to see his grandfather's diary published has been fulfilled.

Robert Nicholson Wyse (1899-1967). The family of R.N. Wyse

Contents

Abbreviations

A/C	Air Commodore
AC1	Aircraftman First Class
AC2	Aircraftman Second Class
A.O.C.	Air Officer Commanding
C.B.Z.	Centrale Burgerlijke Ziekeninrichting, or central public hospital
C.O.	Commanding Officer
F/L	Flight Lieutenant
F/O	Flying Officer
M and D	medicine and duty
M.O.	Medical Officer
N.C.O.	Non-Commissioned Officer
ORs	other ranks
O.T.U.	Operational Training Unit
P/O	Pilot Officer
P.T.	physical training
R.A.F.	Royal Air Force
R.A.F.V.R.	Royal Air Force Volunteer Reserve
S.I.Q.	sick in quarters
S/L	Squadron Leader
S/M	Sergeant Major
S.M.O.	Senior Medical Officer
V.D.	venereal disease
W/C	Wing Commander
W/O	Warrant Officer

Into Battle

Robert Nicholson Wyse was born on July 23, 1900, in Newcastle, New Brunswick. In 1906, the family moved to Moncton, where his father operated a large and successful store on Main Street. The family was prosperous and well connected, and the Wyse home at 204 Cameron Street was something of a social hub in the city. The six Wyse children attended Wesley Church (their father had chaired the church's building committee) and went to the local school; one of their classmates was literary scholar Northrop Frye, whose family home was just behind the Wyse house.

When the First World War began, Robert and his older brother Harry were too young to enlist, but, in April 1918, after they had come of age, they both joined the Royal Air Force (R.A.F.). Neither of them saw action, but Robert's appetite for the military life was whetted. Twenty years later, in part to escape an unhappy marriage, Robert Wyse left New Brunswick for England and, on January 10, 1938, enlisted in the R.A.F. His age made him unsuitable for pilot training, so he trained as an air gunner and flew as a rear gunner on Wellington bombers. After spending almost a year on operations, he was converted to a fighter controller, tracking incoming German air raids and despatching British fighter aircraft to meet them. This safe posting wasn't to last.

The Wyse family around 1905: (from left) Harry Ogilvie, Agnes Annie, Robert Nicholson (at rear), James Wilson, Ruth Osborne, Robert Nicholson Sr., Lyle Smith. A sixth child, Elizabeth, was born later to Robert Sr. and his second wife. The family of R.N. Wyse

Wyse's new unit, 232 Squadron, had been formed at Sumburgh, Scotland, on July 12, 1940, and spent the next fifteen months patrolling the skies over northern England and the North Sea. Re-equipped with Hurricane 2Bs in the summer of 1941, 232 Squadron was considered a fresh unit when the decision was made to dispatch it to another theatre of operations. Four squadrons — 17, 135, 136, and 232 — were assembled into 267 Wing, with orders to proceed around the southern tip of Africa to Iraq. Their ultimate destination was secret, but was rumoured to be either Tunisia or the Caucasus, where they would help shore up Russian defenders against the German invasion. The squadrons were split up, with the commanding officers and experienced pilots posted to one ship and the rest of the pilots, aircraft, and ground staff dispersed among other vessels.

Robert Wyse, 1918, shortly after enlisting in the Royal Air Force. The family of R.N. Wyse

Pilots in training, 1918: (left to right) Robert Wyse, unknown, H.A. Henderson, unknown, Harry Wyse. The family of R.N. Wyse

On December 6, 1941, Robert Wyse and the ground staff of 232 Squadron boarded the *Warwick Castle*, a passenger steamer of the Union Castle line, and joined a thirty-two-vessel convoy that was headed south. Not long after the *Warwick Castle* left port, the blow fell in the Pacific. On December 8, 1941 (a day earlier in Hawaii, across the International Date Line), Japanese forces attacked Pearl Harbor, Malaya, Hong Kong, and the Philippines, achieving stunning successes everywhere. Within a month, Hong Kong had capitulated, Japanese divisions had captured most of Malaya and threatened Singapore, and Manila had fallen, forcing American units to withdraw to the Bataan Peninsula to await relief.

With the situation growing more dire by the day, 267 Wing received a change of orders. A few days before Christmas, it learned that 17, 135, and 136 Squadrons would be sent to assist in the defence of Burma, while 232 Squadron (with a few straggler pilots from 242, 258, and 605 Squadrons) was destined for either Singapore or the Netherlands East Indies. They spent Christmas in Cape Town, South Africa, then headed north into the Indian Ocean. As they approached the Netherlands East Indies, the convoy split, half going to Singapore and half (including

Right: Robert Wyse, as he looked on his first pilot's licence. The family of R.N. Wyse

Below: Area of southeast Asia attacked by the Japanese in December 1941. Mike Bechthold

Wyse's vessel) to Java. At the time, Wyse considered himself lucky; his opinion would soon change.

Japanese forces had leapfrogged from the Philippines to Borneo and Celebes, and their next objective was Sumatra. Wyse and his fellow airmen, after four days as tourists in Batavia, were transported across the Sunda Strait to Oosthaven, Sumatra, where the Allies had cobbled together a mixed bag of British, American, Dutch, and native soldiers to defend the island. Despite its numbers, it was hardly a formidable force. The British anti-aircraft units were well trained, but some had lost their ammunition to Japanese shipping strikes. The Dutch had plenty of small arms and a few tanks, but were also making do with homemade armoured cars. Most of the Allied aircraft available were obsolete, and the best of them, the newly arrived Hurricane 2Bs, had to be uncrated, assembled, and air tested before they could go into action. Most of the modern aircraft available for the defence of Sumatra were concentrated at two locations: P1, once a Dutch civil airport, with two all-weather runways and good dispersal facilities, but no accommodation for air or ground crews; and P2, a huge grass clearing surrounded by a thick jungle of rubber trees that provided excellent natural cover. To Wyse's frustration, there was almost no early warning system, forcing controllers to rely on information from naval units and the well-meaning but ill-prepared Dutch Civil Observation Corps.

Even with these weaknesses, one must marvel at the inability of the Allied forces to mount a strong defence. Japanese paratroopers landed at P1 and the nearby oil refineries at dawn on February 14, 1942, and within twenty-four hours the Dutch commander had ordered all Allied forces in Sumatra to withdraw to Java. Late on February 15, the Allies began crossing the Sunda Strait, and by the seventeenth, Sumatra had been completely evacuated. The withdrawal was clearly premature — the Japanese paratroopers numbered fewer than five hundred, and even with larger infantry units landing nearby, the Allies enjoyed a significant numerical advantage — but it was entirely typical of the mishandling of the campaign in the Netherlands East Indies.

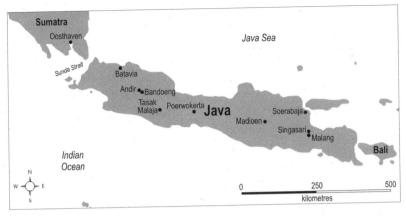

The Netherlands East Indies islands of Sumatra and Java. Mike Bechthold

Back on Java, Wyse and the other airmen had two weeks of enforced idleness. It was not until March 1, 1942, that the Japanese resumed their advance, with a number of landings along the north coast of Java. Again, the Allied resistance was pathetically feeble. The pilots of 232 Squadron eventually were amalgamated with the survivors of 242 and 605 Squadrons into a single unit, but the Allied air force was whittled down every day, losing pilots and aircraft that could not be replaced. At noon on March 3, 1942, the composite squadron was ordered to pull back to the airfield at Andir. At the same time, two other groups of British, Australian, and American soldiers and airmen, numbering roughly eight thousand personnel, were concentrating at Poerwokerta and Tasik Malaja. But on March 8, 1942, with Batavia in Japanese hands and the capital city Bandoeng about to fall at any moment, the government of the Netherlands East Indies capitulated. The Allied units were left with no choice but to surrender as well. With that, Robert Wyse joined the roughly one hundred thousand British, Australian, American, Dutch, and native personnel in captivity.

* * *

Robert Wyse's original typescript diary runs to some sixty thousand words. In editing it, I have deleted passages that were obviously added after the war, as well as repetitious sections. Aside from correcting the spelling of personal and place names and introducing a standard format for dates, times, and ranks, I have left the text just as he wrote it. For example, I have left unchanged terms such as "Japs" that would be considered racist today. To alter them in accordance with modern sensibilities would be to give an inaccurate picture of the world in the 1940s as it was perceived by Robert Wyse and people of his generation. I was also particularly determined to retain Wyse's more frank assessments. He was a man who didn't suffer fools gladly, and was sharply critical of some of his fellow officers, whom he accused of being inefficient, coddled, and self-absorbed. He had nothing but praise for others he encountered, especially the pilots he sent up two or three times a day and a number of the doctors who selflessly treated the prisoners. Sadly, it has not been possible to identify all of the individuals he mentions, but I have added explanatory footnotes where information was available. As much as possible, the full names and ranks of individuals appear in the index.

Chapter One

Malang Prison Camp

Following the Allied surrender, Robert Wyse entered a world of almost unimaginable suffering. Despite Japanese statements that they would observe the spirit, rather than the letter, of international law in dealing with prisoners of war (P.O.W.s), they flagrantly violated the most basic tenets of the Geneva Convention of 1929, established to protect combatants in captivity. Letters to and from prisoners were destroyed or packed in sacks and forgotten. Parcels of food and medicine sent by the International Committee of the Red Cross, which could have saved countless lives in the camps, were left to rot in warehouses, right where Swiss-chartered ships had delivered them. Escape attempts, which were permitted under international law, brought the most brutal punishment. Prisoners were subjected to appalling medical experiments, and were tortured or executed on a whim. There are even documented cases of Japanese officers cannibalizing their prisoners. Wyse would watch, on almost a daily basis, as his captors demonstrated a complete disregard for the lives of their prisoners. The typical guard, it soon became apparent, delighted in inflicting pain on anyone or anything, and seemed to have no moral compass to control his behaviour.

All prisoners, even the officers, were forced to work at jobs that were hard and dangerous, and the Japanese expected a certain number of labourers to be available each day; it didn't matter whether they were healthy or sick, as long as the right number of prisoners presented themselves. For the unwell, it meant spending time in the makeshift hospital, usually on decreased rations — because the Japanese believed that a P.O.W. who didn't work didn't need to eat. The able-bodied faced long days of back-breaking labour in brutal conditions. Thousands of prisoners were, quite literally, worked to death.

But the biggest killers were malnutrition and disease. As Wyse often observes in his diary, the Western digestive system was ill-equipped to cope with an Eastern diet. Rice was a staple in Java, but it was usually accompanied by meat or fish, vegetables, and fruit to provide the necessary nutrients. The P.O.W.s, in contrast, received only small quantities of rice, and precious little else. Occasionally it was raw rice, which was relatively healthy because the vitamin-rich husks were still on the grains, but most of the time it was processed rice, and often of very dubious quality. Wyse, as an officer, had better access to fruits and vegetables to supplement the rice, but even in the best of camps the prisoners were plagued by a host of deficiency diseases that were often grouped together under the term avitaminosis: pellagra, wet and dry beriberi, blindness (caused by a deficiency of fat and animal protein), Singapore foot (in which the soles of the feet became unbearably prickly and tender), and Singapore scrotum (also known as electric balls, it inflamed the scrotum and caused the flesh to peel off). Dysentery and scabies were epidemic, and malaria was a constant threat. It is hardly surprising that Wyse's diary reveals an obsessive concern for food and physical condition.

Allied soldiers, probably Dutch, surrendering to the Japanese on Java.

Collection of E.P. Smith

March 9, 1942 — One hundred percent parade to start our imprisonment. While lined up, a large formation of Jap bombers and fighters appeared. Although everyone knew the war was definitely over, there was a move in the ranks to take cover.

March 10-30, 1942 — There was no water laid on [in] this camp. We got our supply from two small streams running through the camp, and I mean they were small: one only about a foot across and a few inches deep; the other not much larger. A few clear days and they dwindled to nothing. We constantly prayed for rain so that we could get a fresh shower bath off the roofs of the hangars. The drome had never been finished and most of the buildings had a roof only. Mosquitoes very bad here and nets of great importance. There were no amenities, and before they could be dug, thousands of thoughtless men were littering up the surrounds. Even when there were plenty of holes dug for this purpose, many lazy people would not bother to walk that far. The atmosphere soon became unbearable. This condition as well as never being able to wash properly and the sudden change to a rice diet soon brought on various skin diseases, dysentery, diarrhoea, constipation, etc. Bites or bruises would soon become seething masses of swollen rottenness. Lack of foresight on the part of officers and men was responsible for this in the first instance. We needed a strong man to lay down the orders and we didn't have one. We have chloride pills for our drinking water, from the two streams previously mentioned, yet I have caught many brainless ninnies urinating in those streams less than a hundred yards above where water was being drawn, to say nothing of erecting a small dam and taking a bath, signs posted everywhere to the contrary. With a bog hole less than 100 feet from the officers' hangar, I had to move my bed space from the door leading to it, as officers would not go beyond that door to urinate during the night. The smell in a few days was something awful.

The Japs knew there were many of our chaps in the jungle and along the beaches and they took the obvious way to get us into camp. They offered the natives 10 guilders for us alive and 20 guilders dead. The natives would not dare to attack us unless they outnumbered us a hundred to one, but they generally caught up with isolated Britishers and in that way reduced the numbers. The Japs were shooting us on sight by this time to discourage escapes.

At the drome there were many planes, all unguarded, and some of the boys attempted to make them airworthy. The Dutch had been using this drome and I could not believe they would have left them flyable. I was asked by three different escape parties to fly their plane for them and refused. These lads were well-qualified air mechanics and had been working on those engines every night for weeks and they claimed they were OK. A Dutch pilot whom I met on one of my outings and who had been flying from this very drome had told me that nobody would ever fly those planes, and I was much more inclined to listen to him than to our own enthusiasts. Somewhat gratifying though to have the boys

Allied units marched into captivity, Java, 1942. Collection of E.P. Smith

seek me out to lead their show. W/C [Wing Commander] Bell[1] had a Magister ready to take the air, he claimed, and was going to carry extra fuel in drums. A Glenn Martin was also being groomed by some men. Then the C.O. [commanding officer] W/C Steedman came out with this fantastic statement to all officers: 'You are not to attempt to escape by aeroplane because if you get away the rest of us will probably be shot,' thereby spreading consternation among those lads who were trying to fight a war. It was our sworn duty to try to escape and not only that but we had to try to obtain as much information re: enemy movements as possible en route. We carried all kinds of paraphernalia to aid us in that escape. Here, in Eastern Command, don't escape; something might happen to the rest of us.

About ninety percent of the officers here have been in the Far East for many years, too long for their brains to be sizzling in the hot sun, and about seventy-five percent of these only joined up in the last few weeks when the trouble started. These fellows are known by all and sundry as 'tea planters and whiskey swillers.' One has only to see them and hear them talk for a short time to become completely fed up with them. All they can talk about is the amount of graft they should have collected.

We would be allowed to write a letter here, according to the Japs, one per month. All handed in letters but there is little likelihood of them ever being delivered. Plenty of snakes in this camp. [An] S/L [squadron

---

1   W/C Gerald Bell was Commanding Officer of 243 Squadron and former station commander of R.A.F. Kallang, in Singapore.

leader] got away with a 5,000 guilder impress [levy]. Our cooking is atrocious. Nobody knows how to cook rice.

Prices jumped 300 percent right away but soon dropped back to normal. In command of several squadrons at various times. The shifting around, nominal rolls, working parties, etc., very boring. Our own seniors can't be of the same mind for more than twenty-four hours at a stretch.

March 31, 1942 — Ordered to prepare for a move in the morning. My party was not included in this shift. Then, at 10 p.m., was transferred to another Wing and ordered to take charge of a party of thirty-one vehicles and a hundred men to take off at 7 a.m.

April 1, 1942 — After many delays, with the Japanese proceeded to the Central Hotel, where we picked up an escort of a sergeant-major [S/M] and four soldiers. We had been told the trip would take two days. My C.O. allowed me three days rations for 100 men.

April 2, 1942 — Ran into trouble in the Tjilatjap area. All bridges had been blown by the Dutch. We drove all over the area looking for a crossing without finding one. Finally back to a place on the south coast where a small ferry was operating. Got a few cars over, one at a time. Heavy current. We camped by the riverside for the night. Water bottles empty and no water. Ordered river water boiled for twenty minutes and allowed to settle overnight. The rivers bring down everything from all the towns and villages located on them, but had I not done this the men would have drunk the stuff as it was.

April 3, 1942 — Spent most of day getting rest of vehicles across the river. Had bath in native well. Night [in] another schoolhouse. Oh, on the first night out two of our lads broke camp and went downtown to a pub and had whiskey, of all things. The next morning I caught it from our escort. Told that in future the Jap soldiers would be on guard and anyone caught out would be shot. Looked on as a great joke by most of the lads.

I wasn't quite prepared to believe it was. It was very difficult to get the true inference from our escort as none of them spoke a word of English. We had perpetual troubles over petrol, for instance. They expected us to run without it, I guess. That night all trucks out of gas. Nips wanted to leave early in the morning. Spent hours trying to convince S/M we could not move without fuel. He eventually got a Nip interpreter. Wanted to know how much we needed. I asked [how] far we had to go. Not allowed to see the map. Told we had 300 km to go. I then estimated 300 gals required. Too much! Then told only 200 kms to go. Whereupon I estimated 300 gals. Still too much gas but they eventually found 300 gals for us. We travelled all that day and in the evening I learned we still had 180 kms to Malang. Fortunately we had some spare fuel in one of the trucks, otherwise I think I would have been shot. I just could not make them understand that motors would not go without fuel and there seemed to be little of that left around the country for the Japs. Nips that had command of some of the stores would not give any of it to another Nip. Vehicles breaking down and others could not keep up. Stuck on temporary bridges, etc. At one time, three of our drivers on a sling bridge. Drivers seem to have no sense at all and the men, all English, are making things very difficult for me. Threatened with death many times by the guard because of the unruly mob who are supposed to be soldiers. I'd like to have them on a station for about two months and, by cracky, they'd listen to me when I spoke. They just can't get it into their heads that we are prisoners of war and can't come and go as we please.

April 4, 1942 — Got through Madioen late p.m. and on to the next town only to discover eight vehicles missing. Jap garrison town. I was reported to a Jap officer because I did not have the respect of the men and could not enforce discipline. I guess everybody the world over knows what discipline in the R.A.F. is, so I was not unduly perturbed, except for the seriousness of the situation and my own neck. Discipline was ten times as bad out here under the hot sun as it was in England and that's saying something. In the Japanese Army the officer is a god in every sense of the word. He is set apart from the ordinary mortal, is worshipped and obeyed by any Japanese other rank. Naturally they do not understand our lack of it and that has been the cause of most of our troubles since becoming prisoners of war. An English officer orders a man to do something and he might be obeyed at a slow walk. A Jap will do it at a fast run after the customary bows and salutes. Jap soldiers always in full uniform. They were disgusted with my fellows for stripping down a bit. One lad nearly lost his head and I don't mean figuratively. I had passed along the word that my orders were Nip orders and were to be enforced by Nip bayonets (not my scheme). Within five minutes of giving the edicts, one of my drivers balked and started to argue. I could see the hackles beginning to rise on a Nip neck. I hurriedly placed him under close arrest, tied him to a seat in the back of an empty truck for all to see, and then proceeded on my way. Oh boy that fellow looked dejected and it went a long way towards sobering the gang. From then on too, I got a little more respect from Dai Nippon. That boy will never believe that I saved his life.

We put up this night at a Japanese Army camp. We were given a stone slab with a roof over it about thirty by twenty feet. One of the missing trucks was the ration lorry, but on telling the Jap commander we had no food he gave us his rice. And the promise of food the next morning. Our food the next morning was a billy of tea. Officers were allowed to sleep inside with Nip soldiers. We declined. Dog, pet of one of the boys, seized by the Jap commander. Invited out to swill beer at two different Nip parties that night, at the point of the bayonet. There were speeches and I had to reply.

April 5, 1942 — The rest of our gang pulled in during the night. Four men left the convoy on escape plans this day. Later heard from Japs they had been captured and shot. My 100 men were somewhat inflated on departure from [Tasik Malaja]. The first night on the road my cook sergeant issued 121 rations. The next morning I took a secret count and found I then had 119 men. I arrived in Malang with 105, five more than I needed, but I told some of the boys to skedaddle as soon as [we] got inside and then when they were brought together some of the camp officers saw to it that I had the correct number. Early p.m. arrived at Malang, and out to Singasari Aerodrome. In Malang the whole town turned out to see us and one got the idea of being a monkey in a cage. I turned over to W/C Welch. Was given No.1 Sqdn., No.1 Wing, under S/L Hardie, one of the tea planters and about a year my junior in service.

April 6, 1942 — Rested all day and made full report on trip to W/C Welch. At this time I forwarded my views on what would happen if the Nippon demands were not met, in the light of my experiences. No attention was paid to me.

April 7, 1942 — My first day at slave labour on the aerodrome. Squitters all day, afraid [of] dysentery. Carry a roll of bumf with me wherever I go. Have been like this for two weeks, including the road trip. Aided by an M.O. [medical officer], of which we are fortunate in having two, F/L [Flight Lieutenant] Forbes[2] and Liddell, both Scotsmen; I was able to get the business stopped after a time — only to turn to acute constipation. I don't know which is the worse. The damn thing has brought on an attack of piles and they are bothering the life out of me.

April 8-12, 1942 — Just a succession of drome, piles, drome, piles, etc. . . . too miserable to jot down a word.

April 13, 1942 — Barbed wire, sentries pacing back and forth outside and inside. Yes, we are being forced to work on aerodromes, filling in bomb holes, drainage ditches, shifting bombs, oil, petrol, etc. Today being a Nipponese holiday we get a day off from the back-breaking work on the drome. A chance for all to do their washing, if they can find any water. Most of them have one suit only now and that very light tropical wear. Usually too dog tired when getting back from the aerodrome to do anything but draw my rice and flop on the so-called bed. Have not been too well recently, to make matters worse. Have already had most of the usual tropical afflictions, on top of an acute attack of diarrhoea. Skin

---

2   F/L F. Alastair Forbes, R.A.F.V.R., was a medical officer at Malang prison camp.

scratches, bites, etc., are impossible to avoid and almost impossible to cure. Each one becomes septic, squirts slime all over the place and becomes very uncomfortable. The chief difficulty of the moment is to avoid malaria and the hot sun. The sun is wicked hot in this country, absolutely scorching.

The boys tried a football game this p.m., No.1 Wing against No.2 Wing. There are approximately 1,000 men in this camp, all ranks. I am a squadron commander of No.1 Sqd., No.1 Wing — about 145 men and six officers. Every meal rice, rice, rice. I've made myself a bed from odd bits of wood lying around and someone gave me a mosquito net at [Tasik Malaja]. I even bought a mattress the other day through the canteen at 4.25 guilders. Two blankets. Also a table of sorts, a little cupboard and a stool, very rough I'm afraid — primitive is a better word. Have a room all to myself by virtue of being a squadron commander. Before buying that mattress my complete kit weighed less than twenty pounds, rucksack, change of clothes, two towels, shaving kit, (my third) mirror, knife, plate, cup, spoon, sarong, slippers, Bombay bowler, and water bottle.

April 14, 1942 — Working on drome all day.
Breakfast — rice and gravy, black tea
Lunch — rice and stew, black tea
Supper — rice and stew, sweet rice (dessert) and tea

Work party of Allied
prisoners, Java.
www.footnote.com

April 15, 1942 — Drome, but had to quit about 10 a.m. Jap ordered me back to see doctor. Have had the squitters since March 25th, nothing to get up ten times at night. Playing hob with the rear end. Singapore foot is very bad and will not heal in spite of all the care I give it. Feet always get wet during the morning dew, then dry and blister before noon. There is little water some days for washing and others none. Many men sick, many still forced to work with horrible skin sores.

April 16, 1942 — The Nippons have persistently asked for 750 men for the working parties out of our 1,000 and to date our C.O. has never sent more than 600. The Nips are getting very annoyed about it and say that our C.O. is not playing fair with them. There will be an explosion soon and I hope I'm not handy when the shooting begins. They had threatened to cut our rations today if their demands were not met and they weren't. The Jap major told us (junior officers) to produce or else. Sent a delegation to the C.O. with this information but he refused to listen to them. At the moment we have about fifty permanently sick, 100 or so on light duty. Apparently it takes another 250 to run the camp and cook the rice. In my opinion we have just too many lead-swingers with a stand-in with their commanders.

Noon — The ration officer came back and reported that the ration had been cut twenty-five percent, just what they said they'd do if their demands were not obeyed.

April 17, 1942 — Bed all day. Couldn't get up if threatened with death at sundown. Guess this is no country for a white man, sick parades running about 150 per day with about another fifty down all the time. Working parties were nearer the mark today; I've been counting them as they go past my open front. It's a pathetic sight — sick, afflicted, hungry, shoeless, all have to go.

April 18, 1942 — What agony! Awake all night, tossing and turning. Up at 1:30 a.m. and off to the makeshift hospital to see if I could get any relief. Might have some psychological effect, the orderly said, in handing over a pill. I still tossed. At 5 p.m. today, call from the doctor. He entered smiling. At last he will be able to make a thorough examination having got hold of a rubber glove. It turned out to be [a condom] which the owner will have no further use of for some time to come. Informed [me] that he can do nothing for me as he cannot operate, no injection apparatus, no nothing. He was very sorry but that I was in for a very bad time.

April 19, 1942 — Still in bed and having an attack of the horrors two or three times a day lasting several hours. Our other doctor brought in for consultation. Internal cyst as well as the other.

April 21, 1942 — Our first death, AC2 [Aircraftman Second Class] Alcock, R.A.F. He had been sent out [to] the hospital in town and died on April 16th. Up for a walk today. Rice ration increased, other items drastically cut. Have undertaken to teach a group of officers navigation. Helps wile away the time. Nights — bugs, mosquitoes, bats, beetles, crickets, coconut flies, flying grasshoppers, millions of them every night. Also snakes, lizards, etc., galore.

April 25, 1942 — Japanese holiday and we must pray for all the Jap soldiers who have died on the battlefield. Squitters seems to be our worst enemy at this time. Everybody gets it sooner or later or in between. Without any warning a man is taken short and has to jump for it up to twenty times a day. It may go on for weeks and is no fun, believe me.

April 26, 1942 — Drome in a.m. C.O. made me stay back in p.m., although supposed to be able according [to the] M.O. My money is getting low. Less than 20 guilders left. Have been augmenting my rations with a little bread and butter, but will have to stop as I must smoke. Can't understand why the Dutch guilder is still in use, except that perhaps the Japs never expected the islands to be handed to them on a silver platter and consequently are not prepared as yet to administer them. Rations seem to go shorter and shorter every day. Yesterday (the holiday) as a gesture they gave us double the rice ration. Rice is piling up in the ration store, as we are unable to consume it, while other items, beans, greens, a few potatoes, etc., only go from meal to meal. Men go back hopefully to the kitchen for more but have to be turned away. The Jap guards are all buying up cameras, at a very low figure naturally. However, they paid 450 guilders for a real good one the other day. Lucky man that had it. He'll live well for a time. We are able to buy (if one has the money to spend) bananas, raw sugar, peanuts, and tapioca root, also candy, native variety. I've been able to buy a loaf of fairly good bread once or twice, 22 cents per, which I share with my batman. Batman in name only now. He's more of a pal. I've nothing to give him in the way of money but he will not quit in adversity as most of the others have. When he gets a little tidbit he shares with me over a little fire we build outside and vice-versa.

April 27, 1942 — Drome half-day. Breaks the heart to see the Jap planes coming and going all day and not be allowed near enough to make a dash for one of them. There are some ominous-looking machine guns around the perimeter track too, which tends to curb one's enthusiasm. What would one do if one got into a foreign plane and discovered all the gauges and gadgets in Japanese characters? Would one be able to solve the riddle of something big enough to get to Australia in a matter of split seconds?

May 1, 1942 — Stomach cramps, headache, diarrhoea, as well as piles. Doctor orders me to bed for three days. At noon today a W/O [warrant officer] and a sergeant pilot were recaptured in the centre of Malang after escaping the night before. They were tied up in the centre of the compound, a 100 percent parade ordered, then they were given an unmerciful beating. One hundred percent parades ordered for every morning and evening in future. Two officers escaped about three days ago have also been captured. The Japs say they will be shot.

May 2, 1942 — New orders. All ranks, officers and men, will salute all Japanese from the highest rank right down to the very lowest at all times.

Another officer punched about today for not standing at attention when approached by a Jap soldier. There are 1,000 British troops on this airdrome. Earlier on, the Japanese had asked for 600 men for work on the aerodrome. Naturally it is our policy to be obstructionists, but anyone with half an eye could really see that [although] they meant business for weeks, their demands for 600 men have not been met; now they are demanding 750 men on the drome. Furthermore, they say that if we do not produce them they will cut our rations. B[ritish] C.O. sent 600 men today plus 150 of our sick, leaving 200 well and strong men in camp. In this way I think he hopes to gain sympathy from Dai Nippon. I fear otherwise. Feeling better today but no appetite. Ate some lunch today, the first in two days.

May 3, 1942 — F/L Gordon and P/O [Pilot Officer] Cheesewright, who left camp about three days ago, brought in today. None of these men were free more than 24 hours.

May 4, 1942 — Bouquets of flowers with the food lorry. The C.O. thinks the Japanese are fooling, trying to give us a scare. We got the scare all right. All four men were executed at 2 p.m. in a dispersal bay at the drome, with all the ranks lined up to watch.[3] I think perhaps our commander will wake up now. He was horribly shaken up when he came back later in the day. The Nipponese doctor sanctions my removal to Dutch hospital in Malang.

May 5, 1942 — Thorough examination by Dutch internal specialist. Put on milk, meat, and potato diet.

May 7, 1942 — At 2345 hours, severe earthquake shock lasting several minutes. Another at 4 a.m. the next morning. We were pitched about on our beds right handsomely.

---

3   The executed escapers were F/O [Flying Officer] Albert Cheesewright, F/L Robert Gordon, W/O Charles Kenneison, and Sergeant Dennis Poland.

May 17, 1942 — Moved to bamboo ward. All Javanese troops have been released. The Dutch officers and men think they will be released soon too. Plenty of books to read (English). Chess, draughts, and cards. Meals, bread, and tea for breakfast; soup, rissoles, spinach, and potatoes for lunch; bread and tea for supper. I have an abscessing fistula, piles, and Singapore foot.

May 24, 1942 — Another severe examination today, not so good apparently. Fistula coming to a head again and, oh, boy, I have been climbing the walls.

June 1, 1942 — A festival time in Japan and our hosts graciously condescended to add somewhat to our rations.

June 2, 1942 — Another examination today, which nearly took me to the cleaners. Confirmed that it is a fistula which is causing all the trouble. They are always aggravated by the heat in the tropics. My foot is better but the piles — hot diggity. Doctor says the fistula will not cure itself and that he will have to operate. There are many snakes and spiders on our lawn here. Just on the edge of the town, killed a six-foot snake yesterday.

June 3, 1942 — Was able to get a pencil today. Donation from one of the men; have been trying to get one for over a month. Ward flooded again, six to twelve inches of water all over.

June 4, 1942 — Rear end still very sore from examination. Noticeable change in the grub for the festival.

June 9, 1942 — Change of guards completed. I had some seven Japanese soldiers in to say good-bye; one would almost think they liked us.

June 15, 1942 — Examination by Dr. Schoorel and he says I cannot go on as I am.[4] He has asked repeatedly for the use of the operating room on my behalf. The Japs do not refuse, they don't bother to answer at all. The doctor says he will try an experiment if I am willing. There are no anaesthetics. Taken to small room on second floor and an orderly set to watch for Nips. In the middle of the operation he had to stop because I could not keep still. I asked for six strong and heavy orderlies to hold me down and in due course he finished his experiment. The piles are greatly reduced, he said, and were not the cause of all my trouble at all. Climbed the walls for the rest of the day.

June 16, 1942 — Still climbing the walls and walking across the ceiling.

June 17, 1942 — Ditto above, developing into upset stomach and bad headache. Asked for some dope and got it.

June 18, 1942 — Haven't had a sleep since the experiment. Money getting very scarce. I am smoking cheap cigarettes at eight cents per twenty, sugar is at four cents a pound and bananas seven cents per head. I think soon that I will have to give up smoking.

June 20, 1942 — Feeling a little better this a.m. The doctors have certainly been doing well by me. Have had four miserable days of headaches, no appetite, etc., and my duties as senior British [officer] have gone begging. Back on temperatures and poultices again — the experiment not so good. Two more patients in on the fifteenth, one dysentery, other infected hands. That makes fifteen of us in the dysentery ward, a room about

---

4   Wyse was likely suffering from two ailments. The haemorrhoids were probably brought on by diarrhoea and exacerbated by the prisoners' being forced to defecate in a squatting position, rather than sitting on a toilet. He was also afflicted with either a perianal or a rectal abscess that formed a fistula, a small, discharging tube connecting the rectum and the perianal skin. This enormously painful condition can be treated only by an operation to drain the abscess.

fifteen by twelve. [Sergeant] Painter, broken ankle; Chappel, dysentery and malaria; Woods, dysentery; Biddulph, skin infection; Watts, dysentery; Drew, V.D. [venereal disease]; another V.D. left last week, Lawton, Professor at Oxford and Manchester, debility; Mahon, skin infection; Scholes, heat; Bates susp[ected] of appendix; [Sergeant] Hood, chronic malaria; Wiltshire, broken back.

June 25, 1942 — Have added to our games croquet and monopoly, both homemade and a good way to wile away the time for the boys. Croquet particularly good for those who are just coming out of casts and putting aside their crutches. Still keeping to about twenty cigarettes a day, principally because no smoking between 9:30 p.m. and 7 a.m. General condition a little better. One of those things greatly missed is the news. It is horrible not to know what is going on in this war-torn world.

June 28, 1942 — Doctor Forbes came in at 11 p.m. with two emergency cases, perforated appendix and a dysentery.

June 29, 1942 — Every man who is nearly well or able to walk somehow ordered back to the camp, twenty-three in all. It is reported there are 100 cases of dysentery at the drome and no beds available for them.

July 1, 1942 — Still in hospital. Two more dysentery cases in today and sixteen more to come whenever [there is] space. Talked to Doc Schoorel today. They are so short of equipment they hesitate to do the operation I really need. Besides, they just can't get permission of the Jap doctor. My piles are considerably reduced and the fistula only gives me a heel after each move. I do that in the evenings and hope to get to sleep soon. However, it is not so serious as it is inconvenient. Had rain for the first time in weeks. In the dry season now — winter. There is no noticeable change in the temp.

July 4, 1942 — Two months in pajamas — not mine, of course, I lost everything. Day or night, summer or winter, a pair of pajamas is all one need wear. My right ear has been acting up again. [Corporal] Gibson, dysentery, hovering on the brink. Dr. Buning asked me to try to work the old psychology on him in an effort to wean him out of his despondency and keep him alive.

July 8, 1942 — Declared a public holiday by the Japs. Visitors allowed in all camps wherein P.O.W.s. There are many rumours as to how this came about. Generally believed in celebration of the taking of the [Netherlands East Indies] by the Japanese, March 8. However, we had many visitors at the hospital. It was marvellous to see women after all these months, and a spot of colour as the Dutch, Japanese, Ambonese, and Eurasian women turned out in their raiment. Many ladies called who had no loved ones in the camp but still had someone here or elsewhere. Everybody was in holiday mood and most optimistic. The English were treated every bit as the Dutch and Lord knows how much was spent on food, candy, cigarettes, cigars, fruits, lighters, etc. I had two offers of money, refused naturally. These people will need all their money in the near future. The ladies stripped their gardens, we had flowers galore. I met a lady whom I had seen in the Hotel Smit, Palembang. We recognized each other on sight. Her husband is a prisoner of war in Batavia. She had brought in a package for one of the English. There were several cartons of cigarettes, many oranges, bananas, tangerines, soap, chocolates, and bars. Doctor Garonwy, Army, senior Navy [other rank], and myself, R.A.F., decided to throw everything into the common pot, as some of the boys being bedridden had not received as much as others. We had a stretcher full of delicacies, including sandwiches, chickens, toothpaste, brushes.

July 12, 1942 — Received can goods and cigarettes from Singasari. Gee, had Heinz sandwich spread for supper. Corporal Gibson not doing very well, more dysentery cases in today. They have to be at death's door before the Japanese doctor will sanction their removal to hospital.

July 15, 1942 — Corporal Gibson, on a rigid diet, left unattended the afternoon of the visit, stuffed himself with chicken and other weird items much to the confusion of the medical staff; now he is much better. The doctors gave him twenty-four hours to live after the feast. Right now he is being washed by a native orderly. He is as flat as a board and . . . his hip bones stand out and his legs near his hips are smaller than my forearms. The other half of our hospital had been occupied by civilians; they were cleared out today. Dutch boy dying in another wing tonight, asked our Welsh boys to sing hymns — these lads had a choir in their battery. I have taken the place of their two basses who had been posted out to the camps. We sang the hymns, although we got into great trouble with our hosts.

July 21, 1942 — More dysentery and scabies in today. Chappel, who only left last week, in again. There is little sleep at nights with the clatter of the bedpans, to say nothing of hobnailed boots and the rattle of bayonets. I think the Japs are afraid to patrol around outside because of the reptilian life in the grounds. W/C Welch in visiting. He tells me that now they hold the sick parades in the evening and treatments at 10 a.m. — what I suggested months ago, to beat the slackers, and save the cut in our rations. The C.O. is singularly averse to taking advice.

July 23, 1942 — Forty-two years old today. Wakened by the good wishes of [Sergeant] Painter in the next bed. He said: 'May you enjoy many of them and for all of our sakes not another in Java.' I received many little gifts of cigs and cigars. Touching, with all the boys so hard up. The Dutch came en masse all day to express greetings.

July 30, 1942 — Howe wins the farting contest . . . breaks all existing records for dysentery patients. Fifty-two moves at half time with twelve hours left to go. Previous record set up by Mahon about two months ago with forty-eight moves in twenty-four hours. Corporal Gibson has won the endurance record with an average of twenty-five moves per day for four weeks. The dexterity of our orderlies in handing out bedpans is beyond compare. Three jumps from a chair to a bed, snatching up bedpan en route, a violent lunge as in sword play, estimated time one and a half seconds, then a contented sigh accompanies the gurgle from the patient. Frequently, you hear: 'Steak-pan! Hurry! Please! . . . Damn it, man, I can't wait all week.' All this between first call and accomplishment, which takes no more than two seconds on the average.

August 8, 1942 — Another visiting day according to the Nips. Friends and relatives came from far and wide, but the Nips would not let them in. Some of the hundreds of baskets they brought were allowed in and I received two for the English.

August 14, 1942 — Inspection by Nippon doctor. All cases able to walk ordered back to Singasari whether they are well or not, to leave on Monday.

August 17, 1942 — Got up and dressed for the first time in 3½ months. Packed my few belongings. The Dutch command was very generous to me, fitting me out with a blanket, shoes, helmet (Bombay bowler), two vests; someone gave me a shirt two months ago, and a water bottle. Dr. Schoorel, 2.50 guilders, a pipe, and some tobacco. Others cigarettes. We are leaving behind twenty-two patients, all dysentery, scabies, and beri-beri. Arrived at the drome before lunch.

August 18, 1942 — Doc Forbes gives me seven days light duty. I had fairly good food and am much better although I did not have the operation I so urgently needed. Have no idea what reverting to the rice diet will do to me. The Dutch surgeons told me on leaving that I was due for a great deal of misery. Today is a *yasume* [rest] day for the troops. My wing, 400 officers and men . . . left over a week ago for no one knows where.[5] General consensus of opinion is that it was Hardie's influence on Welch which was the cause of our ration cut and most of our troubles. Glad to be rid of him. He was all bull and bluster in the privacy of his own

---

5   This group was the first of nearly 2,500 Commonwealth P.O.W.s sent to build an airfield at Sandakan in Borneo. Only six of them survived the war.

room, but he never came in contact with the Nips, never went to the camp office, or to the aerodrome. The Japs have performed a miracle in making one of the 'destroyed' Fortresses fly.

Moved in with Fitch and Abbott. They both have plenty of money and I have none, which makes it very difficult. They are augmenting their rations quite handsomely. Water scarce here. No taps, no showers. Brought in on trucks in barrels by Nips and naturally never enough to go around. Blackout in town and being practised here. Natives working here now, not enough fit British.

August 25, 1942 — On light duty today but it is Nip *yasume* day. Men unable to wash clothes because no water. Soccer games in p.m. Not so pleasant being with Fitch after all. He is very self-centred and like many Englishmen has no respect for anyone else's feelings or thoughts. To hear him expound one would never put him down for a clerk in a carpet shop. No sign of a move for us yet but things look like one in the near future. No ill effect as yet from the rice. I am augmenting with yams now to replace bread and bananas. Yams are very cheap. We call them yams, although they are merely the roots of the tapioca. They taste something like sweet potatoes and one can make a meal for five [with] one cent's worth. Plenty of papayas but I dare not.

Typical work assignment given to prisoners in Java: moving things from place to place as drawn by Dutch prisoner Andrew van Dijk. Collection of Jan Krancher

August 26, 1942 — Took company to drome for the first time in four months. Miraculous change. Hangars cleared. New runways finished. Bomb holes and drains filled in and now finishing tarmac, perimeter track on connection roads. About 1,500 coolies employed now doing the same labour as white men. Maybe they don't like being on a par and they take every opportunity to gloat. Came back to barracks with meaty toes, violent headache, and a recurrence of my old trouble, to say nothing of blistered heels.

August 27, 1942 — Resting today, headache not far off. Suggested to doctor that I do half days for a start. I must have rest or else. The Japs tried to get my cigarette lighter again today. They confiscated all cameras today and ask for a price on them. On their being overvalued, as they claimed, they are taking them for nothing. Water very scarce, we are in the middle of the dry season. Temperatures over 100 degrees every day and no rain for over a month. Winter but I don't find the heat unbearable. Acquired a pillow. Woodford retained my bedroll while I was away. I'm making some alterations to shirt and shorts which were given to me in Malang. Soap going scarce, 25 cents a cake now and way out of my range, I only have Doctor Schoorel's gift of 2.50. The camp is agog with rumours — wherever these things come from, God only knows. About two months ago in this camp they had it that the Yanks had recaptured all of Java but Malang Aerodrome. They were even laying bets on how soon they would be freed.

August 28, 1942 — Was at drome for half a day. It is a filthy, dirty, dusty place now in the dry season and the work going on raises dust. Tractors, trucks, shovels, coolie baskets, steamrollers all contributing. Absolutely played out at noon. My affliction demands plenty of rest and good food. I don't get the latter obviously, but only such b— as these would insist on my working when it is so unnecessary. There are many surplus officers here who are young and fit; the Japs only want eight out per day of thirty. My exhibit is quiescent now but dear knows how long that will last, and the doctors here know that there is no treatment or an operation to be had for me. Have contracted a skin disease (boils).

August 30, 1942 — Drome today, came back played out and as dirty as a pig with no water to wash in. We have been rationed to a half gallon per day per man, all purposes, but the non-workers grab all of it before the workers get back.

August 31, 1942 — Told 3 p.m. moving in the morning. Kit inspection at 4:30 p.m. Many more of our precious belongings taken by the Japs. Fitch in a spot of bother. In packing he has acquired a truckload of antiques and art through his job as canteen officer, gifts by kind-hearted people in town to the poor English prisoners, which he reckons the poor English prisoners won't want.

A typical prison camp (albeit a very tidy one) — sketch Andrew van Dijk.

Collection of Jan Krancher

Chapter Two

Lyceum Camp, Soerabaja

The destination for Wyse's party was Jaarmarkt, a large facility that had been the site of Soerabaja's annual trade fair before the war. But their time in Jaarmarkt was short, and within days they were moved across town to the Hogere Burger School, a residential school (not a seminary, as Wyse notes in his diary) that was known to the prisoners as Lyceum Camp.

September 1, 1942 — Hurried into lorries at 10 a.m. and departed shortly after, no waiting around with the Japanese. Lovely drive through thickly populated country to Soerabaja, the largest sea port in Java. Our prison here is a former race course and fairgrounds, thick concrete walls, sentry boxes at the four corners, and guards perpetually patrolling through the *atap* huts.[6] Every Nippon guard seen even at a great distance must be saluted or bowed to, and one must stand rigidly at attention until they are out of sight. Another search of our meagre possessions on arrival, very thorough and much more of our stuff taken. Saw a small British flag being stamped on. About 1,000 British troops here already, about 3,000

---

6   *Atap* huts are made of nipa palm leaves woven onto bamboo frames.

Dutch, some Australian, American, and all other nationalities represented. Managed to get some bed space on some bamboo raised up from the ground, most of the troops on the ground here, but it is the dry season.

September 2, 1942 — Practically no outside labour here. The camp is horribly dusty and dirty but fortunately there are a few showers. The bog holes are a seething mass of microbe life. Wing Commander Cave's party went to Batavia in March and they are here now, many officers and men that I knew.[7] P/O Shutes . . . offers 5 guilders for my lighter. Woodford advises me to keep it for a better price.

September 3, 1942 — Getting used to it but this is pretty hard living. Food even worse than at Malang and not so good for a Westerner. Small piece [of] bread in the morning with a cup of tea, bread very heavy and soggy. Lunch, boiled rice. It is generally too well cooked, naturally with no sugar, salt, or milk. Supper, steamed rice, a small ladle of stew (so-called), no fat, no sugar. With a cup of tea, no accessories. That's all there is, there ain't no more. At the canteen you can buy cigarettes only — understand they used to sell tea and coffee.

September 4, 1942 — At noon today informed of another move, don't know where but think old English to be sorted out and confined together. Trying to sell my lighter at any price, sorry I didn't take the five guilders, am stone broke. The Nippons had allowed us to keep some of our English iron rations. Now the C.O. is giving us each a share. I had a share in a can of apples, a small spoonful, a half a can of bully beef and an eighth of a tin of potatoes — that, with my noontime ration, à la Dai Nippon, made one good bellyful. A small cake of soap, invaluable now as there is none to be had. P/O Shutes paid 3.50 for a tin of bully three weeks ago. The Dutch went into internment apparently with advanced knowledge. They have money, clothes, and all the personal comforts. They had heaps of time to make prisoners of themselves as the Nips

---

7   W/C Norman Cave was commander of R.A.F. radar units on Java.

did not catch up to them for several weeks. We have also divided up our welfare money from Malang, about which two-thirds got through the search. A bag of sugar disappeared and it is said the Dutch are paying 5 [guilders] a pound for it. Our erks [aircraftmen] are raising Cain over this sugar. From the canteen I received 20 cents and roll of toilet paper which the W/C insisted I should have because of the aforementioned experiment; three-and-a-half-cent packages of cigarettes, a package of shag, a quarter package of chocolate, and a small cake of soap, one quarter package of salt, two small packet of tea, worth about one penny.

There is damn-all charity between the British prisoners of war. Never in all my life have I seen such examples of selfishness. There was a riot over a case of corned beef, several boys injured. [Just] a spirit of 'the hell with you, Jack, I am looking after myself.' Officers and men alike sit in front of others and fairly gloat over food that they have been able to purchase. When the capitulation came, huge impresses were handed out to officers for disbursement and the common good, [but] large sums of it remain in their own pockets and those of their friends. Tonight I sold a pair of socks, a gift, which I do not need, for 2; also a half cupful of petrol for 1. Our *atap* huts present a lively spectacle tonight as the Dutch come from all over to buy up the few remaining possessions of the English. I don't know who wins. Our lads need the money for food, they certainly don't need many clothes in this climate, but we have been at great pains to issue them with shirts and shorts to cover their nakedness, and the minute they get a new shirt off they go to see how many guilders they can get, guilders of course representing food.

September 5, 1942 — Breakfast: a small piece of bread. Fall in at 9:15 with any baggage one wants to retain and can carry. Roll calls on the *padang* [parade ground] in the blistering sun, move off at 11. My assortment of junk weighs about 100 pounds. It depends on how long the journey whether I reach our destination with all that. Guards lining the streets as we shuffle along, a motley crew, officers and men staggering along under impossible loads. Everyone wants to take as much as they can on to the next camp. Arrived at our new home about 1 p.m., the streets were like infernos, and it was shattering to hear the bugle calls for lunch hours before we reached there. Searches until three o'clock, during which we were not allowed to accept drinking water from English already there.

Dumped into a room twenty by twenty which is scheduled to take twenty officers. It is not so easy the way these selfish people do it. The men, of course, can put forty in this space without any trouble. A draft came in here some months ago in the middle of the night, pouring rain. The Japs kept them in the mud for three hours, then gave up the count in disgust and left the prisoners in the darkness to find their own shelter. One of the officers on waking the next morning in this very room counted sixty bodies other than his in various attitudes on the floor. Needless to say, in some instances they were lying two deep and the stench was something awful. I had saved half my bread from the morning ration and I sure appreciated it with water as soon as the parade was over. One is getting inured to hunger now. The rice diet is never satisfying, for although at times I get an opportunity to really stuff myself, yet a few hours later I am almost famished. I find that the best way to combat this is to lie down and not exert oneself in any way.

There is water laid on here and plenty of taps, but they have cut the pressure and one can only get a mere dribble. Doc MacCarthy[8] says it is supposed to be drinkable and it had better be, for it is the first time I have taken water unboiled in over six months. Have to drink it here as there is nothing else. There are a few wog toilets, supposedly flushable, but we are not allowed to use paper for fear of clogging the drains. We must now change to the bottle, native fashion. Nosing around on arrival I found a plank bed abandoned by a Dutchman, also a few sticks for my mosquito net and aided by an erk got it moved into my room. Others were afraid of draughts so I got a four by six spot under a window (110 degrees in the shade) and am quite comfortable.

---

8   Aidan MacCarthy was an Irish doctor who joined the R.A.F. in early 1939 after being unable to find work in civilian medicine. He survived over three years in captivity, spent the rest of his career in the R.A.F., and died in 1995.

September 6, 1942 — Minor changes in the diet at this camp. Breakfast: pap . . . and a cup of tea.[9] Lunch: a small square of bread something of the consistency of a Firestone tire and not quite so edible. It is made of rice, tapioca root flour, perhaps a little wheat flour added, but that is very doubtful now as they do not grow wheat in this country. Supper: steamed dry rice with a small ladle of stew (the colour of dishwater and just as thick). Some of the most amazing things get into that stew. Sometimes one can detect a faint trace of the ground-up meat that goes into it, but very seldom. Proof in the fact that one needs no soap to wash the *blik* [mess tin] after this meal. It is generally a watery mess, unflavoured, flat to the taste, but it wets the rice and makes it go down easier. Officers and men will go to any lengths to augment this diet, seldom possible here. Working parties going outside the camp can sometimes pick up a few items of food from the natives if they have a lenient guard. Smokes are almost unobtainable. They have to be rationed equally. In the old days under these circumstances a friend who did not smoke would pass his ration along to you. Now, he can ask and get any price for them, and the man with the most money can live like a king. On arrival here a fellow officer asked me to change a 2.50 guilder note. I did, giving him the equivalent in Japanese money. Half-hour later, the same officer told us that the Japs accepted nothing but Jap money in this camp, and sure enough they won't. Christian charity! Having gone to extremes in sacrifice to acquire a few dollars, I now have some stuff that is no good. I have a half packet of pipe tobacco left, but had to stop smoking because of ulcers.

I think our new place [is] better than the last one. It used to be a priest's school, takes up one city block in the residential area. Across the street from us on all sides are lovely Dutch homes, set in shade trees. My window is only twenty-five feet from freedom. We are left pretty much alone in our internal organization and only the R.A.F. could produce the utter chaos we find ourselves in most of the time. Sanitary conditions are

---

9   Pap was a rice porridge that had virtually no taste and virtually no nutritional value.

unspeakable, mostly the fault of our own men, who just can't be bothered going for a bucket of water to flush with. The camp is full of shade trees and surrounded with conifers, many beautiful lotus trees among others.

September 7, 1942 — The days slip past quite rapidly in spite of the monotony. Seems to be a combination of rice, bread, rice, sleep, and repeat. A very few turns around the *kampong* [village] tires one out. Must be getting weaker as never in my life have I suffered from the heat, and I have spent many years in hot climates — must be the food. Smoked my last cigarette last night.

September 8, 1942 — Jap holiday. Collected a new bunch of grief by trying to smoke a weird combination of dried grasses, etc., in a donated pipe. Woodford, my former batman, is still able to produce the odd cup of tea from somewhere. No milk nor sugar, of course, but highly acceptable. We are horribly overcrowded in this camp. Dysentery is epidemic, we have lost five already.

September 9, 1942 — Nippon inspection at 11 a.m. Sold two packets of Gillette blades to friends at 25 cents each, Canadian price. I could have charged one dollar a blade. I got them from stores abundant in Batavia. I now possess one guilder Japanese. Inoculation for typhus, cholera, and dysentery at 2 p.m. W/C Steedman, W/C Groom, A/C [Air Commodore] Silly, and nearly all high-ranking senior officers have been gradually weeded out and taken away. We have been all questioned many times on pertinent things and do not know whether these people are going to funeral parties or not.[10]

September 10, 1942 — Arm infected from inoculation. The doctors themselves don't know what the serums are. It is a fact that the Nippons are scared to death of dysentery. Twenty-five hundred men living in this

---

10 W/C Edward Steedman was executed by the Japanese on May 15, 1942, at age thirty-seven; A/C Benjamin Silly died in captivity on December 7, 1943, aged fifty.

city block, all one-storey sprawling buildings with their red tile roofs, typical of Java. Jammed in together are English, Americans, Dutch, Ambonese, Chinese, Australians, New Zealanders, to say nothing of one lone Canadian. All English-speaking troops in Soerabaja are now in this camp. And the conditions get worse. There is friction between the Ambonese and the Dutch, the former are fighting men of great heart. They are real tough and they figure the Dutch let them down. In fact we all do.

I rose early this morning and did a large *dhobi* [laundry]: shirts, shorts, singlet, socks, towel, [mosquito] netting, and two handkerchiefs. Quite a task when one can't spare any soap and water is very precious. All out on the grass now and I'm looking forward to lunch, which is still hours away. I could eat the side off a cow and all I'll get is a small piece of bread. Had balance of two tablespoons of sugar given me from the canteen at Singasari, I shall use a few grains of it in each cup of tea. Woodford gave me eleven cigarettes. Wouldn't tell me where he got them and I am smoking three a day. Time of writing I have two left. All the bedbugs in the camp made a run for Jordan when he arrived, and he is only two beds away from me. He is the dirtiest grown-up man I have ever met, seldom bothers to wash and never takes a bath. He blamed S/L Hopkins for bringing the bedbugs in. He wailed on the subject repeatedly, and so far Hoppy has failed to recognize his existence. What better answer than silence? Everyone knows he killed 130 in his net this morning, he counted them right out loud. Today, about one week after arrival, he has decided to clean up his makeshift bed and get rid of them. I came from *dhobi*-ing and found all his bedding piled up in my space. I hit the roof.

September 11, 1942 — A few turns around the *padang* last night, completely worn out, slept well. Took a pee in my drinking mug during the night rather than walk a half mile to an overflowing latrine. There is a queue at lat[rine]s and cans twenty-four hours a day. On our last move, much baggage was left on the *padang* at Jaarmarkt camp in the hope the Nips would find transport. They did, for what was left of it, the Dutch having stolen most of it in the meantime. The Wing had some sugar in bags — the bags arrived filled with sand, for instance. Everything edible had been taken. We had been getting a teaspoonful of sugar in our pap once in a while. I picked up four five-cent packages of cigarettes last night. Corbett, non-smoker, was selling me his cigarettes; has now decided he can get more in trade elsewhere. Another tea planter. Days continue hot and dry. Well over 100 in the shade and possibly 130 in the sun. It's so hot nights that you spread yourself out; if a leg touches a leg or an arm the perspiration starts pouring down.

There is a scramble daily for the long, bean-like seeds from the lotus trees. Boiled, they taste good, a sticky, sickly sweet mess. A monkey captured at Singasari brought along as a pet now feeds in the foliage of the many trees and goes flying madly through the treetops having the time of its life, always returning to its master at night to sleep cuddled up with one arm around his neck. Three Ambonese were beaten up badly by the Nips last night. They were caught talking to their wives through bamboo. The wives were brought in by the guard, humiliated, and made to witness the spectacle. Can only manufacture a move every second day now on the reduced diet and it is causing me trouble. The experiment is acting up, I'm afraid.

September 12, 1942 — Parted with my lighter for 10 guilders, exactly what I paid for it seven months ago. Bought magnifying glass for fifty cents, which gives me lights eleven hours a day, and 9.50 in change. Have not been beaten up for three weeks, a record. Am touching wood. The first five minutes with a bowl of rice is spent digging out all the maggots.

September 14, 1942 — Another nominal roll today. Playing some bridge for a change in the afternoons. I warned these fellows but they will persist in playing for money. The extra pennies get more food to me.

September 15, 1942 — Did my washing early and over to Woody to dry. Only a 100 percent parade saved the works. Woody got it too near the

One of Robert Wyse's few souvenirs from captivity: the knife
with which Dr. Forbes removed his cyst. The family of R.N. Wyse

barbwire and a guard started to throw it over the bamboo
fence. If you put anything out to dry you can't take your eyes
off it for one second. Odd remarks heard about the camp.
P/O Corbett: 'he had never met an Australian who would
make a good officer, the Aussies as a whole were worthless.
. . . If the Nippons had guaranteed to leave Malaya alone,
it would have [been] better to give Australia to them if
they would keep the Australians.' Such ingratitude — I've
never seen the like anywhere of these Malayan *tuans* [mas-
ters or gentlemen]. And to my way of thinking there's not
tuppence ha'penny worth of brains in a carload of them.
Self-centred, conceited, arrogant, incompetent fools, practically all of them. They only joined up in Singapore in
order to get out of the country ahead of the advancing Japs,
now they are wailing their heads off because they are under
military jurisdiction. They claimed that they would much
rather be interned at Singapore. Singapore complex, we call
it here. Too many years in an enervating atmosphere has
almost completely sizzled away what few brains they might
have had when they came out East. If they could only see
themselves as others see them they might hesitate to con-
demn unseen a very fine people.

September 16, 1942 — Nippon inspection set for 10 a.m.
then 12, 3, 5, as usual. No one cares about the inspection
but rooms once cleaned cannot be entered again until the
business is over. I have more money now than I've had
in five months, but they have stopped our canteen and I
can't spend it. The small bite received a month ago is now

festering rot about the size of a half-crown. Getting thinner every day and less energy to expend. My ailments as a whole, though, not bad, so I shouldn't complain. Memories are going and I can't seem to concentrate on anything for any length of time.

September 17, 1942 — The belly has gone bad again, sore for weeks.[11] It broke open in the showers again tonight and Dòc Forbes decided to hack it open. Was that knife ever dull. As a sop to the dull knife he gave me some kind of a pill and succeeded in removing what he called a huge cyst. I shall remember that operation as long as I live. The stuff he took out of that thing seemed to include everything but the kitchen stove. I didn't realize it was so bad. Forbes balled me out for not coming to him sooner, but I've had so many complaints this past six months that I hardly noticed this thing.

We have had our sugar and rice ration cut, to what extent I do not know. We were getting a spoonful of sugar about every third day. It seems strange that we have to suffer for lack of food in a country that exported millions of tons of food per year and which can grow everything under the sun. Deliberate starvation is the only answer. At most of these prison camps one can look through the wire and see bananas, papayas, coconuts, pineapples, sugar cane, yams, a multitude of food going to rot in the trees and fields while we are practically starving for vitamins, anything to offset this pernicious rice diet. Practically everyone is suffering from beriberi now. Sanitary conditions are abominable, holes filled to overflowing and completely stopped up. One still has to go. Endless queues on the few still working.

September 18, 1942 — Umpired a makeshift game of baseball for some Yanks. Had a handful of tobacco given to me and handed it on to Woody, who was out completely. He was treating me to cigarettes last week.

---

11   This was probably an abdominal wall abscess, possibly an infected sebaceous cyst.

September 20, 1942 — Homesick, blue, tired, hungry, dirty, sick, and sore all over. I think the church bells ringing this morning [at] a little native church across the street made me feel homesick. Also out of cigs. The bells rang out in a subdued tone — funereal is a better word. In England that was to be the invasion warning — the peeling of the church bells — and that reminds me that I never heard the church bells in England. Today and all days I experiment with my bread. I try to keep a few mouthfuls for the next meal in the hope of having one stuffing at that time. I masticate the stuff slowly and can stretch it out to about an hour, but the difficulty is to stop when about halfway through, with the belly still howling. Oh, first of all, I get my loaf and look at it for a half hour. During the afternoon, one's mind keeps returning to that small mouthful which you have saved and if anyone can go until suppertime without touching it under [the] circumstances, he's a better man than I am. To be hungry is bad; to be out of smokes as well is something unmentionable.

September 21, 1942 — Lecturing to a flock of officers on navigation. Have Singapore foot again and damnably sore. Still no smokes and suffering. Some lads raffled off 250 tins of cigarettes yesterday. Original cost 1/3d. They sold 700 tickets at 10 cents each. Today they are millionaires. Today a box of cigars (50 cents). Sold 500 tickets at 10 cents, for a net gain of 49.50. There ought to be a law against that.

September 22, 1942 — Cracky! My bridge and navigation students got together and gave me a huge wad of shag. About half a pound, I believe. Another guy gave me 20 Mascots. There is a Santa Claus. AC1 [Aircraftman First Class] Lane, a stage manager in [England], is going out on a working party tomorrow. He is poorly, so I gave him enough money to buy himself a good stuffing if the Nips allow. With luck he might smuggle in something for me. Good lad. I had to give him 20 guilders some time ago. Am in the constipation stage at the moment. If it isn't diarrhoea or dysentery, it's constipation. The doctors say that on our restricted diet a move every fifth day is quite sufficient. Having dizzy spells quite frequently. The sick parades are growing longer each day. M.O.s are appealing for clothes, rags of any description for bandages, but of course no one has anything to give away now and remain decent. Everybody has some kind of an ailment, and the doctors, having nothing to work with, try to stall the men off as best they can. What we, the English, have done to warrant the treatment we are receiving at the hands of the Japanese, I can't say, but one thing is sure, if something doesn't happen soon there are going to be a great many dead Englishmen in Java. There are numerous cases, even among the officers, who have given up all hope, despondent, living in their own dirt and showing no interest in anything. When I reach that stage, no hope for the future; if I recognize it in myself, [I'll] cut my throat. This is the 200th day of my captivity, if I can still count. No one ever dreamt that it would last even 100 days.

September 23, 1942 — Tried some baseball again this a.m. Expect to get stopped any day, as the ball frequently rolls under the wire and the Nips dislike to bestir themselves. The barbed wire is about five yards inside the bamboo fence. The Nips don't like baseball now — keep us waiting hours for the ball — because it is an American pastime. A sub-lieutenant of the Royal Navy caught it this a.m. for not saluting properly. In self-defence he raised an arm to protect himself — fatal.

September 24, 1942 — Umpired this a.m.; too lazy to play. Two natives tied up to the trees in the forecourt this a.m., their screams had rent the air all through the night. It is said they tried to escape the camp. If so, they have had it. I hope they do the shooting elsewhere, it is so depressing to witness an execution. Glory! Got five packets of cigs today.

September 25, 1942 — Had a few words with an English officer who was helping himself to my tobacco in my absence. He of course laughed it off; I call that thieving and a very serious crime at a time like this. If he'd asked me for it, I'd have given it to him and have treated him many a time. This is my thanks. He knew where it was hidden. No doubt he is a very responsible man back home and the incident is alarming. We must be deteriorating. The two escapees wired up to the trees, one an Ambonese, the other a Sumatran, decided to try to break camp to call on their wives, who live in the town. They had only just got through the barbed wire when caught. They were given bread and water at noon today, the first food since their capture. They had been taking terrific punishment every hour around the clock as well.

September 26, 1942 — Received through the canteen today two cakes of soap. One of these cakes would last for one bath at home. Here it must last for months, all purposes. Washing one's clothes is merely a rinsing and a light squeeze, else they will fall apart; then a bleaching in the sun. Dust and dirt. One can seldom get even the body clean.

September 27, 1942 — Getting noticeably thin and weak. Many dizzy spells daily. A great deal of air activity over the town last night. Many new guards in this camp. Two natives still tied up and look a sorry sight. Had to stand in a queue forty-five minutes this a.m. with acute diarrhoea. Yesterday a.m. had a few sips of tea, black, but with some sugar in it. How wonderful it tasted.

September 28, 1942 — The natives were given a *blik* of rice in the evening. They look very tired; stand with heads bowed most of the day and night. As soon as one goes down the guards gather around and beat him till he rises. We were called for a 100 percent parade this p.m. and I thought it would be to witness the shootings, but nothing happened.

September 29, 1942 — Starting the fifth day of the natives' torture, so they may be freed later after all. Had a few sips of sweetened hot water this p.m. We were issued with a small quantity of coconut oil which is to last a month — two [ounces], or about one inch square. One is apt to measure time by such things as when we got the chillies with the rice, or when we received our sugar issue, a spoonful etc., rather than by the date or last Sunday. One says, almost spontaneously, it was the day of the last sugar issue. Erk badly burned in the cookhouse last night in moving a huge cauldron of boiling water. As there are no oils or treatments for him, it can be fatal. Erecting a birdcage on the *padang* today.

September 30, 1942 — Being out of salt for some time, I screwed up enough courage to ask P/O Jordan for some. He has many huge lumps of it in his kit. Knowing the meanness of most of these fellows was the cause of my hesitation. He replied that he had plenty of it, yes, but he was keeping it for trading purposes as money was of no use to him.

The natives are still alive. Watched two medical orderlies dressing their wounds last night. As soon as the orderlies were out of sight, the whole of the Jap guard turned out for some amusement. The general scheme seemed to be to work the dressings off the wounds with sharp pointed bamboo sticks and then prodding the points into the dirt, [to] see how far they could work the dirt into the exposed wounds. These wounds had been caused originally by poking sharp sticks into their flesh.

General inspection by a Jap colonel. These things are proceeded by about a half-dozen inspections. First the duty soldier takes a look around, then the corporal, next the N.C.O. [non-commissioned officer] of the guard, then the sergeant, the sergeant-major, the camp commandant, usually a lieutenant, then we have the local colonel, and at long last the visiting officer. A general inspection slated for 10 a.m. usually ends up somewhere in the middle of the next week. The idea being to see, I think, just how much of a nuisance they can make of themselves. One would think that some good would result, that someone would note the filthy conditions around the camp, the overcrowded hospitals . . . but nothing is ever done about it by the Japs. Much conjecture concerning the birdcage being constructed in the far corner of the *padang*, right under the sentry box. It is of barbed wire, about six by eight by seven feet.

October 1, 1942 — The Japs have changed the guards completely, and the old guard put on a special display of hate to show the new ones how we should be treated. The reign of terror has been going on for several days; anything we do is wrong, whether right or wrong, and the result is many beatings. The question of the birdcage has been answered. Today the two special prisoners were led out to the cage and installed within. Now it seems it is the duty of the sentry to keep poking his bayonet or sharp sticks at them during each tour of duty. Another stunt is to make them stand for hours on pointed stakes driven into the ground. If they do not comply with every indicated demand, the guard enters the cage and beats them unmercifully with anything he can get his hands on. A few days ago I watched these prisoners when they were tied by wire to the tree in the back of the guard house. I stayed there for hours to compile a record for this log, revolting as it was; and having seen with my own eyes I now hesitate to put it down. It would be much easier for those poor fellows to die at once, but the Japs are infinitely more subtle than to allow them to. In order to fully punish them they must keep them alive, and they go ahead with the torture with that in mind. The guard changes every hour, and the whole guard every twenty-four hours. Whenever the duty guards march in and are dismissed it seems to be their duty to add a little more to those two men's suffering, for they immediately come out and pick up the rude bamboo sticks and commence abusing the men's bodies. Some of the things they do are obscene and just could not be put in print. No part of the body is inviolable. When the guards have tired of their amusement they retire to the shade grinning like monkeys, and the prisoners if still conscious gain a respite until the guard changes again. If they fall down during this procedure they are kicked to their feet, kicked in places that makes it imperative for the man to get to his feet. If he faints or loses consciousness, other prisoners are called to bring buckets of water to revive him, then the business starts all over again. I . . . it looks as though these fellows are going to be allowed to live, and one wonders if they will maintain their sanity.

I shall have to give up lecturing navigation to some of my friends, I believe. Last night I had a simple little problem to explain and found that try as I might I just could not make the grey matter cope with it. It was laughable and my boys had much fun at my expense. They say that they are experiencing the same difficulty. In other words the memories are failing. Horrible thought! It's the awful food and the steaming atmosphere. I have come to saving all my butts for resmoking. I hope I don't fall so low as to go around the rooms and grounds picking up butts as one of our eminent officers is doing at this very moment. He is being very cagy about it and hopes that no one is aware of what he is doing. Sick parades now running ten percent of full strength and over every day. My doctor is one Dr. Thompson, a vet. Or sanitary inspector, I think. He certainly doesn't know the first rudiments of medicine.

Caricature by Dr. Leslie Audus of Dr. Alastair Forbes, the physician who treated Wyse.

Dr. Leslie Audus

October 2, 1942 — Much to the consternation of the above I asked for a transfer back to Dr. Forbes and got it. He is much better and a very hard worker. All days are alike, a perpetual round of bowing and saluting our little yellow hosts. No one goes near the *padang* any more for exercise as it is too revolting for words to see what goes on. Jordan, who refused me salt, asked to be allowed to use my wog bottle last night. I refused. Too much danger of dysentery. The man hasn't a brain in his head. S/L Hopkins fainted on *kiotski* [attention] this a.m.; from his bed to attention was too much for him. One has to climb to the perpendicular very carefully. On our last 100 percent parade about 100 fainted in the hot sun. Managed to acquire a little salt and am rationing myself to a small pinch per day. One can understand the value of salt in the desert or back country. Soon there will be none in camp. Also, one can more readily understand the washing of feet in biblical times. We live on the floor or near the floor, wear sandals or clogs which must be removed when we enter our billets, otherwise the situation would be hopeless in the seas of mud and dust. On the draw this day pulled the smallest loaf and am frightfully hungry.

October 3, 1942 — Have made a little box to collect my spoonful of sugar in, so that I can save half of it until the next day. The new guards seem to be shuffling about the street outside all night, and what with the changing of the inside guard and the continual harsh shouting that accompanies it, one can hardly get a wink of sleep.

October 4, 1942 — Another Sunday. Will one ever hear those church bells ringing back home? The church bell across the street rings dolefully every Sunday morning and causes much introspection.

October 6, 1942 — This is sugar day. Will try to make mine go three days this time. What a hope. We are not allowed to sing or whistle any more. Some kids outside the fence went past whistling 'Wings Over the Navy' and the Japs recognized it. They later returned singing 'God Save the King' and received a severe beating. This was apparently taken for a means of communication. Farthest from our minds. In fact we have nothing in the way of news at this camp, consequently we have nothing on our minds at all except to keep as fit as possible under the circumstances and await that day of delivery.

October 8, 1942 — Three cases of diphtheria in the camp. Have a small isolation ward in the northeast corner. Have to start P.T. [physical training], two sessions of fifteen min. per day. It will be a hardship for many . . . I have hopes that I am becoming accustomed to the rice diet. Even look forward each meal hour to a few more mouthfuls and don't just have to stuff it in while practically holding the nose all the time. I came away from the doctor's attention for the first time in six months today. Bowels have been normal for some days, fistula quiescent and Singapore foot not too bad, cyst as well. In fact am feeling better than at any time since capitulation. If people in the Far East can exist on rice there is no reason why Westerners can't do so as well in time.

October 10, 1942 — We now have four parades a day. Morning and evening *tenko* [roll call] and two P.T. parades. Doc MacCarthy stepped from the back door of the hospital to collect a few towels from a line. A Nip was hiding behind a tree and as the Doc did not see him and failed to salute, he received a bad beating. Protests are useless, one just has to stand at attention and take what's coming. Dutch money is no longer legal tender. It's a wonder it has remained good for so long. The Nips will exchange anything we have to their own stuff, thank heavens. No rain since June, I believe, but [it] will be coming soon enough — a mixed blessing, purifying and yet endless seas of mud. This afternoon in giving salute to Nippon S/M, I called 'canary' instead of *nowarie* [*naore*, or as you were]. Difficult to remember all the Jap words. Fortunately this bloke was in good humour and took it as a joke, only poked me on the nose a few times. Inoculation for plague today.

October 12, 1942 — Am rationing myself to one pinch of salt, one pinch of sugar, and twelve drops of peanut oil per day. No amount of rationing will keep me in cigs and tobacco. We are not getting them at all. This is a tobacco-growing country and there should be plenty. Am very sore from inoc[ulation]. All Nippon money now, but as we can't buy anything it doesn't seem to matter. Listened to a talk by Lieutenant Commander Hughes on the Far East from a naval point of view. Interesting to discover that chaos existed in the Navy as well as the Army and Air Force.

Japanese-printed money for use in the occupied territories. The family of R.N. Wyse

October 14, 1942 — As I anticipated, having to stop smoking is the greatest hardship of them all to endure. Every little incident becomes magnified. One becomes irritable and hates to associate with one's closest friends. Our meagre food rations accentuate the loss of this mild drug. One is in a perpetual sweat, can only lie down and think about it and stew. A quiet soothing smoke is an aid to enduring hunger, discomfort, and now that has been taken away from us. Our last order was for eleven cases of cigarettes and we received three and the Nips took one of these at our expense. A Chinaman just in with a carton of cigarettes wants 1 [guilder] per packet for which he paid five cents.

October 16, 1942 — Had a cigarette issue yesterday, my share eight cigarettes, two weeks since I saw one, and as this was only an aggravation I smoked them all at once. Corporal Ross, a London Scotsman and a fine fellow, died yesterday of dysentery. Holding an inside burial service for him, very impressive. Saw two white women in the guardroom yesterday, the first in many months. One never thinks of women now, there are too many real troubles to face.

October 18, 1942 — The Nips sent four magnificent wreaths to the funeral service. They are very good in this respect, sometimes even sending the wreaths before the victim has expired. A canteen has finally come in. For 25 cents my ration is one [kilo] sugar, quarter [kilo] salt, quarter [kilo] coffee, one package of tobacco at 60 cents. These are the precious things. Spirits around the camp much higher as a result, and the Nippon guards seem to have tired of beating us up. If they only knew how harmless and how willing to please we all are. All our troubles are from misunderstanding of Nip orders. They are always searching out trouble. And when one gets beaten up himself, he immediately comes inside and takes it out on some prisoners.

Washing is one hell of a problem, no soap, one dare only rinse or the things will fall apart and the best one can ever get is a flannel bath. After a tremendous effort I managed to save a whole loaf of bread for the poor period, which started yesterday. The worst loaves are only one-third the size of the best, which are still very small. With fourteen drawing in my room I have one good week and one poor one. One can buy a loaf for 25 cents and one's rice ration. Robbing Peter to pay Paul. Some of the raffles are quite fantastic. Why the senior officers allow such things to go on is beyond me. Some of the Ambons who do not smoke will pool the tobacco and cigs they draw automatically. They easily sell from 300 to 500 tickets at 10 cents each — 30 to 50 guilders for an article that cost them 60 cents. The Americans caught on and this is their scheme. You can buy a 5 cent package for a guilder. Twelve guilders for the carton, which they now raffle and collect 40 or 50 guilders. Inflation! I have sworn time and again not to buy and so have most of the others, but when one has not smoked for weeks and gets a chance to acquire a carton of cigs for 10 cents, it's pretty hard to resist the temptation, no matter what he thinks of it as a swindle. On one of these Yank swindles yesterday I paid one-third the price of the article for one chance in 150 to get it.

October 21, 1942 — I don't think it can be any hotter than usual but it feels as though it were. Sweat, sweat, day and night, and unable to wash properly. The flies are very bad in this camp and with the open drains, presage dire events to follow.

October 24, 1942 — Out of a blue sky we were called to the office last night and paid. Must be the Geneva Convention getting to work. At long last I am a millionaire. I drew 125 and am now wondering what to do with it. Have a rotten cold and am barking all day and night.

October 28, 1942 — Went outside in charge of a labour party yesterday and got a bit of a break. Taken to a Nippon Army camp on the other side of town. Nice to see the town and some people in fine raiment. The colours do make a decided contrast to our sorry lot inside. Dutch, Eurasian, and Indonesian women had seen us pass through the town and at noon came from far and wide with baskets of food for the prisoners. I had fifty men in my party and every one of them got stuffed to the gullet. Every man Jack of them brought back his bread ration, which had been issued before we left and which was to have been our lunch. Every man had one egg, two tomatoes, two oranges, six bananas, a good stew with rice, and a can of sardines, beans, corned beef, and fish all mixed together. There were a few sandwiches and cakes, a can of concentrated milk, coffee, sugar, and three tins of milk. My first milk since May 1 in Malang hospital. There were papayas, cigarettes, and cigars, candy, etc. Our guards gave us ice water a.m. and p.m. and in the afternoon went one better with some iced rose water. Half-hour rest both morning and afternoon, during which our guards passed us cigarettes (unheard of). The Nippon [sergeant] in charge was very pleased with the work of my men and said so and that is the reason for the above, I think. It was just like a real old-fashioned picnic back home. On return to camp, were issued with double rations because we were a labour party and none of the boys could eat it. It wasn't thrown out. Woodie got all my extras and did he wolf them down. He is batting for me again at 50 cents a week. I have some money to pay him a decent wage now but he won't take it. This lad is the same through plenty or adversity. We share everything, has been the standing rule for many months. Another death today — dysentery. Was completely played out last night when I returned and have been resting all day. Never have I tired so easily. Becoming quite expert on rolling my own — when I can get some tobacco.

October 29, 1942 — Another death today — typhoid. The Nippon No. 1 comes to all the funeral services, receives many *keireis* [salutes], takes a bow to the corpse, and departs. Night before last we got two bananas for supper, tonight a piece of papaya. A canteen came in. I received about one [pound] of onions, four red hots (chilli), about half-pint of ketchup. They say there are some soya beans for the kitchen, and two [packets] of shag and two cakes of soap per man. We have started a fund to get extra food into the camp for general distribution among the men. Our room put up 270 guilders, or about 20 guilders per officer. As far as I am concerned they can have all mine except a little cigarette money. I shall try to collect it after the war. On receiving my donation from the Nips, thinking there must be an error of some kind I put most of it out among my boys, who are poorly. They are to keep it until all danger of my being beaten up over it has passed, then use it to buy themselves food. What with my 20 [guilder] donation to the fund I am almost broke again, but I got enough vitamins a few days ago to last me a month. We have many beriberi cases and the whole lot of us are potential cases, so that anything we can beg, borrow, or steal in the way of food will help to stall off the evil moment. All our deaths to date have been caused by lack of food. The bodies had no resistance to combat disease. The Westerner cannot exist on rice alone.

October 30, 1942 — Had a magnificent meal last night — added chopped onions, ketchup, and salt to my stew. Dessert a piece of papaya and finished with sweetened coffee. Not forgetting the rice. Best meal I have had in months except for that working party. As we pay for it ourselves, I can't see why we don't get the opportunity more often. As we have 126 beriberi cases, our dysentery ward full and discharging patients early to make way for others, our hospital wards full to overflowing, hundreds of others queuing daily on the sick parades, hundreds of others sick in quarters and unable to move. It is inconceivable that something will not be done soon about giving us more food, more particularly our own kind of food. No matter what we have received for food to date, it has been equally shared out to every man whether he has money to pay or not, and of course ninety percent of them are broke. Having some money coming in, now I can do my share regularly. The millionaires never did anything for any of us.

October 31, 1942 — And the rain comes. Already the camp is a quagmire. Mud up past the ankles anywhere you go. Clogs off is the order of the day. Every corridor and entrance is being used by prisoners for bed space, even under the eaves outside they will be found with all their earthly possessions in a very confined space on the floor. As they all have to keep their places spotlessly clean, they dislike having any mud tracked through. All very difficult, as one hates to dive into the swamp every time he must make a call. The one campfire allowed in the camp is just outside our door, and the smell of frying onions is overpowering for one who has never eaten an onion in his life until the other day. Never again will I turn up my nose at anything edible.

November 1, 1942 — Two more deaths yesterday. Things are getting serious. Still have an awful cold, but would not dare complain when there is so much distress about. The aforementioned experiment is giving me trouble as well. Ordered by the doctor to do nothing but attend 100 percent parades. Our pet monkey has turned out to be a destructive little beast and should be destroyed. Oil issue today, seems to have shrunk to insignificance in the face of other delicacies received recently. Woody in bed now. Singapore throat and ear. Some of the lads have been trying to kick a football around, resulting in four broken arms in a few weeks. Ordered stopped today. The men lack the vitality necessary for such hard exercise, but will just not be told. A few days ago we were inspected by a Nippon big-shot who had been a prisoner of the English in Australia. Exchanged. We are hoping that he will organize the same kind of food and treatment for us that he received there. Not a day passes without some poor chaps getting pounded unmercifully for no good reason. The rains are now coming in earnest and conditions are horrible. Impossible to dig any more bog holes and the ones in use are all overflowing into the compounds. The psychological reaction of officers, supposedly of some intelligence, after eight months' confinement is worthy of note. The only way to get along with them is to remain silent under all circumstances, no matter what the provocation. Never venture an opinion, sing, whistle, or make any kind of racket. If one does, one is immediately squelched. One can hardly say three words without starting an argument which might develop into a free-for-all fight. Whatever plan is adopted by the higher ups for the distribution of foods or the general running of camp affairs, that plan is always wrong and calls for hours of vindictive discussion almost amounting to sedition, riot, and mutiny. Nerves have apparently reached the breaking point.

November 8, 1942 — Sick parades still mounting and dysentery is epidemic. The lavatories dug just outside our door are partly responsible, I believe, along with the crowded conditions. We are doing all we can by advertising to make the men dysentery conscious. Signs all around the camp with illustrations. We are in the midst of a squitters epidemic as well, and as the medicos have neither microscopes nor slides, they cannot tell what the affliction [is] until much too late for an early cure. Fit bodies create a toxin themselves to combat dysentery; not so the unfit, and who among these is fit today? Then, after deciding that it is dysentery, they still don't know which kind, and if they did, it still makes no difference as they have no medicines.

We had been augmenting the existing rations out of our pockets; food was coming in through the canteen. But now the Nips have seen fit to stop the canteen for some unknown reason. Also, officers will only receive 10 guilders of their pay per month. That is to stop us feeding the men, I guess. The Nips say our rations are sufficient. The remainder of our money is accounted for thus: 42 guilders for food and lodging (we actually worked out the cost of our ration to be about 2 guilders per month on today's prices), 18 guilders for amenities (we dig our own in the ground), and the 55 left is placed to our credit in a Japanese bank outside. We had hoped that by pooling the resources of all the officers we could raise the existing ration to a level which would lower the sick ratio, but that is not to be. It looks like deliberate murder to me. The Nips are aware that the bodies are being carried out of this camp much more frequently as the days go by.

November 11, 1942 — Armistice Day of the Great War, and one's mind crosses the oceans and pictures the march to the cenotaph to pay homage to the ones who passed on at that time. When this war is over, [I] will be among the marchers or the dead. Depressing thought and not to be entertained for a minute. Yesterday we were ordered to write a letter and discuss three things — 'English ignorance of Nipponese abilities, our good treatment as P.O.W.s, and our desire to return to our sweet homes.' Only a Westerner could guess the assortment of baloney that was turned in. Six officers are down in my room out of fourteen. One company of 230 men has 143 men sick or having treatment. We are experiencing a terrible epidemic of squitters, and as it has been raining continuously, the victims are enduring the tortures of the damned. Men stagger to the holes outside and have to stay there for hours. Flu and colds rampant too. Clothes soaked, bedclothes damp, and almost impossible to find a place for them to dry. My conjectures concerning the rainy season were all at sea. I pictured the lovely warm spring rains back home, not a torrential downpour that even comes into the billets. One would certainly welcome a bit of the blistering hot sun today. Started for the showers, so-called, last night and had my shower before I arrived. I was glued to the spot in shin-deep mud while the rain came down in buckets. Have received a small issue of tea and cocoa, also one and a half [packets] of cigarettes. Have been able to dispose of 85 guilders of the original 125 without getting into trouble. Put it out in 10s and 15s to fellows who have been on their backs for months.

November 13, 1942 — Rain, rain, rain. Everything soaked. Haven't done my *dhobi* for weeks. Up four times last night to pee. Medicos say it's not kidney trouble, it's the diet. On speaking to one of them about it, he asked me how many times I had been up during the night. On telling him he said: 'What the hell have you got to worry about, I was up six times myself.' Changing shoes, clogs, sandals, wading through the mud to the latrines. Slogging through it all day to pee, almost hourly after tea and pap in the mornings; out in the rain for food, 400 yards to the cookhouse and another 400 back, slipping and sliding all the way. Our fire outside almost impossible to keep going and yet we must, because leftover bread and rice must be cooked to reduce the possibility of dysentery.

November 15, 1942 — Received an issue of tobacco, with the compliments of Dai Nippon. Extraordinary! I am well supplied at the moment and smoke a pipe mostly.

November 17, 1942 — Two more funerals today. One of them was a grand boy whose bed space was just outside our door on the veranda. He was nineteen and the sole support of his mother. Only ill one week. Was as clean living a lad as [was] ever born but his body had been undernourished for many months and could not throw off a minor illness. His buddy lying alongside of him was carried off to the dysentery ward yesterday and he was so depressed over the loss of his pal that he doesn't want to live. Still dull and raining and a cloud of gloom has settled over the camp because of the many deaths.

November 18, 1942 — Sun shining for a change. Bed clothes out and *dhobi*. Inspection day as well. There is much dissension and bickering among the officers; it goes on morning, noon, and night and takes in from the highest-ranking officers to the lowliest P/O.

November 19, 1942 — My trouble returned in full force yesterday. Started with the morning inspection parade, which took three hours. Up at 6:45 and on parade until after 10 [inches of] continuous rain on an empty stomach. Doctor's edict four days S.I.Q. [sick in quarters]. On my visit to the hospital I find that there are more than eighty there now. The hospital is a shack at the far end of the compound which was abandoned as uninhabitable during the rainy season. It is full of dysentery patients. Two hundred and thirty-seven S.I.Q. and besides there are hundreds calling at sick quarters twice a day for treatment of all the tropical horrors. And now bedbugs. I have been able to keep reasonably clear of them to date although surrounded. Yesterday being inspection and wash-up day, several of the bedbug habituals decided on a massacre. Result — they scattered them far and wide by the thousands and the poor things of course went looking for new blood. I remained on my bed all day beating them off from all directions, including the ceiling, and ran up quite a score. This morning, on taking my clothes out for an airing, I shot down many more which have lodged in my net. Later in the evening while entertaining friends, one of the little brown fellows strolled across my blanket, much to my embarrassment. Crabs and itch in the private area is very prevalent. Corporal More died today.

November 21, 1942 — Two more deaths yesterday. Seven had gone out to C.B.Z. [*Centrale Burgerlijke Ziekeninrichting*, or central public hospital] the day before, one dying shortly after arrival. We've been getting together some cat walks through the mud with a few fair days to work in, also organized some large utensils for drying our rations — needless for everyone to get soaked every meal. I've been getting thinner. No way of telling but I must have lost from five to ten [pounds]. Won't go much more than eight stone now.[12] Still have a rotten cold; I'm barking most of the night. Find it difficult to concentrate on anything for any length of time.

November 22, 1942 — Another death today; that makes six in the last six days, I learned at the hospital this a.m. Now that I'm drawing a little money I can help a few of my friends among the other ranks. We have been told that we can order food through the Japs if we have the money on the spot to pay for it. We put through a blind order immediately. Now we are making up a colossal order and hope some of our tightwads will shell out. A new disease of the mouth and lips is spreading around — lack of vitamin C, the doctors say. Cankers, ulcers, sores all over the inside of the mouth and throat. Wheat and oats are now impossible, there being no imports for over eight months and these things are not grown in this country. Dysentery is the biggest bugbear. We have started a war on flies and all that, but it goes on increasing.

November 23, 1942 — Sugar issue, three-quarters [of a] kilo. Another death today. According to Doctor Thompson, tonight there are over forty sick in hospital and in billets and over 700 on the sick parades every day. And these parades are increasing daily. The medicos are becoming quite concerned. There have been fourteen deaths in our two months at this

---

12   A stone, an English measure, is 14 pounds.

camp — attributable to lack of food and crowded conditions. The Nippon colonel made a speech to the troops yesterday, he realized we were crowded, but the buildings were good and houses scarce. (The town is practically empty.) We should get plenty of exercise and sun, other camps were the same. He was perturbed at the report of two deaths yesterday and expressed his sympathy. The Nippon Army was working in the interest of humanity for the world.

November 24, 1942 — Another death. Cigarette issue, thirty cigarettes.

November 25, 1942 — Another death. Much air activity both day and night. Half-packet of tea issued today, and I have quite a store. I have been drinking cocoa, mostly for health reasons. Had a bad night. Musical instruments returned by the Japs. The Nip colonel told us to exercise on the *padang*, but every time we venture out there the guards find an opportunity to do some baiting, which ends in a general beating for anyone in the vicinity; consequently none of the boys will go. Besides, there are the two in the cage and it is not pleasant to see what happens to them.

November 26, 1942 — Another death today. Tiny Mason is keeping a complete record.

November 27, 1942 — Ambons and Chinese are being moved out of this camp today, over 300 of them. Thank God! There will be more space for our men. Perhaps we can get most of them in from under the eaves and from the verandas. Found a dysentery Ambon working in the kitchen. Ambon died today. An awful storm through the night. Back on M and D [medicine and duty] now and must attend all parades. We are trying to build a shelter over the cookfire outside, with poor results. Bridge and navigation lectures have fallen through because of sickness. Have acquired an assortment of boils and blisters all over the neck and shoulders.

November 28, 1942 — Our room is to move to the other side of the camp. Better outlook over there, no smoke from the fire and no bog holes right under one's nose. Breaking up our communal mess. Glad to see the last of the Philadelphia lawyer and 'Gloomy Gus.' Gus is [an] S/L who lives in his own filth, the world's leading pessimist and was never known to smile. Born in China, English public school, farm in Kenya. He is twenty-four years of age, good for nothing, engaged to a perfectly charming young lady, and is utterly devoid of anything in the way of ambition. He is an officer in the Royal Air Force who openly states that he didn't join up to do any fighting, he only joined because it was the thing to do. I have watched bedbugs crawling all over his mattress and on pointing them out to him he would squelch a few of the many and let it go at that. He doesn't mind them, he says. He raised Cain, however, when a crabs suspect sat on his bed.

November 30, 1942 — Heavenly day! A banana and an egg were issued today. Informed that perhaps our food order might come through.

December 1, 1942 — Orders to move to another prison camp in a naval barracks about five kms away on the outskirts of town.

Prisoner in Java attempts to cook a meal for his hut mates — sketch by
Andrew van Dijk. Collection of Jan Krancher

Chapter Three

Darmo Camp

December 2, 1942 — *Padang* with bedroll at 10 a.m. Fall in at 1:30 with pack — stand by for search. I lose nothing as I have nothing of value left. Move out into the road after search and commence marching at 2:30. This march was made in the hottest part of the day, on the hottest day I have ever known and, in fact, the hottest day our Easterners had known in years. I have no idea of the temperature in the shade and we had no shade, just hot pavement all the way. One hour and a half without a stop and into a new camp, where we blistered in the sun on the square for hours during another search by our new guards. The troops on the whole behaved real well. Started singing — were stopped — whistling — and were allowed to continue. Any waving or talking to Dutch women on the streets would produce dire results for the guilty one.

December 3, 1942 — Speech on early parade by garrison colonel, who stated that we had been moved for health's sake. There is more sun in this camp, no shade trees and a wider aspect but all the buildings are drab *atap*. Toilet facilities seem to be better; they are the wog, flush type.

Overleaf: Murray Griffin. Interior view of 100-metre hut, Changi, 1944, brush and brown ink and wash over pencil, 37.4 x 53.6 cm.

Australian War Memorial (ART26492)

Quite a number of showers. Food about the same, but we had placed some food orders at Lyceum Camp and some of them came in the day we left. I saw cases of sardines and tins of milk. I got one-third of a jar of peanut butter the night before. All our table knives are taken from us here. Mine was tin and utterly useless. I'm parked in an old room [with] four old friends — that is, prison camp friends; knew none of them previously. Had a mango at noon, the first I've seen and tasted — marvellous, similar in taste to a sweet juicy carrot though stringy. There are flies in this place by the billions. Organized fly swatting has no effect. Medicos must go after the breeding sources. Another death just before we left Lyceum, Ballinger's corporal. Have an end room and a corner space, grabbed a bed and a wizard shelf and clothes hanger, nails and wire for net and everything. Wonder of wonders. A few letters have arrived here from Africa for some of the troops. Does anyone know that I'm a prisoner of war? Perhaps I shall get a letter some of these days.

The evening count was made by the Jap commandant. He was sorry that we had so many sick in our ranks. While in his camp, [we] would obey orders or we would be punished. The move was made to help give us back our strength. Here we would get more sun and air. Our doctors must work hard. The men themselves were the prime factors in the combatting of disease. We must keep our bodies clean without water. The bread knives which were seized in the search the day before would be loaned to officers only by the Nippon Army. We would be punished severely if they were lost. There are 480 Ambons and a few Dutch here.

December 6, 1942 — Our cooks have been taking a few lessons from the native cooks, apparently, for the stew was much better than I have ever tasted in a prison camp. But there is never enough of it. None of the food orders have shown up and everybody is hungry. One chews his ration of food in the queue and looks longingly at the stuff being handed out to others before moving off. The Dutch officers here have camp life well organized and apparently get along well with the Nips. Our English officers have never been able to approach anything near them for amicability in this respect. W/C Welch, C.O. here as well as in Malang, is always antagonizing the Nips in his every word and attitude. He has done this right from the start and it does no good. We cannot escape. We have to suffer imprisonment and indignities, but conditions could and would be improved by the Nips if they were approached properly and in the right spirit of submission; even a temporary submissiveness under the present circumstances would work much better than his detached attitude of disdainful acceptance, which only a supercilious, ignorant, bombastic, overwhelmed with his own importance Englishman could adopt. Both junior and staff officers have remonstrated with him time and time again to no avail. He is the senior officer here and we are all a bunch of nitwits. That's all there is to it. At times we have suffered unnecessarily because he refused to ask for things of the various camp commandants. We didn't get extra food at the Lyceum Camp because he would not put the orders through. When Doctor MacCarthy was beaten up he would not write a letter of protest. W/C Coffey, senior M.O., did it himself, asking protection of the Red Cross. I just can't figure the man out. I know he is not afraid of death. We were all threatened with death at Singasari — that is, senior officers and squadron commanders. He didn't give a hoot about that, but he is the type of man who always rivals the other fellow in conversation and is definitely not the leader of men.

W/C Vines, next in seniority, is an absolute washout; has been playing sick since capitulation. He had something to do with the Malayan Air Force, but is absolutely hopeless as a soldier or a leader. W/C Walker, Equipment, a hopeless milksop — posh London clubs are full of this type of well-dressed gentlemen of leisure. W/C Cave is the next; he is the guy who put up the black in the train smash. He is just a pot-bellied, perfectly harmless nincompoop. We have nine W/Cs here and many S/Ls. The other W/Cs are so far down the scale in seniority that we never see them except in the food queues, and one can only judge them by their greediness and their desire to grab everything they can use their rank to get for themselves.

And speaking of greediness and senior officers brings to mind our padres, all squadron leaders. We have five or six of them here. It is not only my opinion but that of many others, officers and men alike, that they are the most avaricious, greedy, grasping, self-centred bunch of swine, bombastic in demanding things for their own comfort, that we have in this camp. God knows there may be one or two of them who are sincere in their jobs and desire nothing for themselves, who give service and make sacrifices for the troops, but I'm speaking of the breed generally. They are always the first in the food queues, that brings them back first for seconds; first in any free distribution, first to grab any clothing, blankets, chairs, beds, etc., wherever we go. After their attempt to escape the island failed, I watched them grab corned beef, sausage, etc. from our precious stores when they had all kinds of tinned goods hoarded in their corner bed space. Everything in the way of rations was ordered to be turned into the camp store. They ignored the order and later explained they thought that only full cases was meant; they had broken the tops off theirs. All of them had money and bought all the delicacies they wanted from the starving erks, who thought they needed [money] more than they needed food. In ten months of imprisonment I've seen only one padre call on a hospital ward. He was so bombastically depressing in his loud talk that the ward heaved a sigh of relief when he left. Three officers whom I was calling on said it was the first time they had seen one and if that was the best effort he made at cheering them up, they hoped that he would never call again. I personally have visited the wards of sick men daily for many months in hospital myself and that was the only padre I ever saw there. They sit around their comfortable quarters and lap up brews of coffee or tea, their special delicacies in the food line, and do nothing. On our arrival here the Dutch officers told us that the Ambonese would sell their bread for 10 cents, [and] not to pay more as they could not eat it anyway. In spite of this, some of our aforementioned friends are paying 40 cents, much to the consternation of the Dutch.

We were paid again for the month just before leaving Lyceum. I got 10 guilders, the balance [of] 105 guilders being taken care [of] for me by the Nips; they say we have good food and accommodation and don't need the money. It makes little difference, as our food orders are not coming in, or if they did they would exceed this amount. We have been moved over here because of our frightening sick parades and the unnecessary deaths which have occurred, but the only thing that will improve our health is more and better food, food that will give us the necessary vitamins. No amount of fresh air and sunshine will cure beri-beri or stop dysentery, malaria, and the various festering sores and rotting flesh that the human body, being so low in resistance because of lack of food, cannot throw off itself or even start to heal itself. All this in a land of plenty. Every conceivable type of fruit is grown here and we never see any to speak of. There are all kinds of cattle, pigs, chickens, sugar, and vegetables. This island exports food, thousands of tons every year; 45 million natives, most of them growing food. The island has always been self-supporting and yet our men die of starvation. On a round of visits here, the men as a whole seem to like the change, so perhaps it's a step up, if only psychologically. The place is much larger in area than Lyceum, on the outskirts of the town and not completely shadowed by huge shade trees. One can take little walks without falling over guards and the inevitable slapping.

December 7, 1942 — One year ago today I sailed from England. I was going somewhere to work with some real fighting he-men. Little did I dream [when] I gave up my posting to an O.T.U. [Operational Training Unit] in Scotland, which I thought was a sissy job, that I would find myself mixed with a bunch of nitwits who would not put [up] a fight if their own homes were violated, including a wife or a teenage daughter. Thank God my conscience is clear and I worked with a few he-men, the pilots, from my arrival right up to the last day. It does not help much though when I think of the absolute muck-up this campaign turned out to be. I have two Malayan tea planters, Scots, with me in this room, along with an ancient S/L. All old soldiers of the last war, and they are all living in the past. Boring at times but they are sincere and were probably very good soldiers in their youth.

December 8, 1942 — One year of war against the Nippons. This morning they had two squadrons of bombers orbiting the town, presumably to celebrate the anniversary. It would make a very inspiring display for all the local natives. Nine months P.O.W. and it looks like many more to come. If one didn't have hope for the future, none of this would be worthwhile.

Our war against the flies seems to be of no avail. Everyone has been killing them by the thousands, but still they come. They are of a particularly vicious breed and will not give up until they land on one's food in spite of any evasive action taken. Put your pap down and turn to get a spoon and the pap is black with them. We have invented every kind of a trap to catch them, made swatters by the thousands, and still they come in ever-increasing numbers. One cannot sit and read, play chess or bridge, or just plain sit without being persistently dive-bombed by them. Bodies streaming with sweat from the steaming sun seem particularly attractive to them, and any kind of a sore is pounced on gleefully by them in swarms. No amount of waving, slapping, or moving about will shake them off.

My Singapore scrotum has become increasingly annoying during these past four weeks. Impossible to describe this diabolical horror of itchiness. It is prevalent all over the camp. Took mine to the doctor and, wonder of wonders, he said he had just the thing to cure it. He did, eventually, but never as long as I live will I forget the agony of the first fifteen minutes after application. One of our tropical thunderstorms [is] brewing outside and if possible there are more flies than usual bothering me while I try to write this log. There are many monkeys and dogs in this camp, owned by the Dutch. One hates to eat a pet! '*Kiotski! Keri! Nowera! Yasume!*' Nippon guards going through the billet, and didn't I have to scram to get this buried. I believe I may have said a few things uncomplimentary to the little yellow B—s in it.

December 13, 1942 — We were shown the *Nippon Times* (printed in English) dated Dec. 8 and the *Soera Asia*, which some of our Dutch friends are able to translate in part. Another paper showing American losses at sea in comparison with Dai Nippon was given us late today. The Japanese Navy apparently has the whole of the American Navy surrounded, sunk, or completely bottled up in home waters. With the

Americans helpless, we the English cannot expect them to send supplies and materials to aid in the war against Germany. Obviously we are losing the war. I really can't begin to figure just who the little yellow blighters are trying to impress.

December 17, 1942 — Band concert last night. Command performance! I mentioned the musical instruments being returned which had been seized earlier. Well, ours were only homemade things and we received by mistake cornets, trombones, altos, everything, including a piano, not too well tuned, admittedly, but nevertheless a piano, and I doubt if any piano could be kept in tune in this humid atmosphere. An order for foodstuffs of ours has also come through. Very welcome. I received fifty cigars, a carton of native cigarettes, half tin of jam, tin of liver paste, kilo of sugar, two bananas, two oranges, two lime, two mango. Our mess of eight got some drippings and a little cooking oil. One of our orderlies produced some marvellous rissoles, also a chocolate blancmange. Now we toast our bread every day. On the whole, if things do not deteriorate suddenly, as they frequently [are] in the habit of doing, we are not too badly off. I must confess that I am getting very irritable, so I never go near anyone or enter into conversation.

Air activities in the early morning hours keeps one awake. Saw a Douglas Boston the other day, must have been flown by a Jap. Had to go back to doing my own *dhobi*. Doctors now say that the Singapore scrotum is being passed through the communal *dhobi* boards. Besides, the boys are tearing my few remaining clothes to pieces. I think they hung my only shirt on a barbed wire fence to dry the last time, the back of it is ruined. Again, with only 10 guilders a month to spend, one cannot afford anything in the way of extra expense.

December 19, 1942 — There is a nice walk here around three sides of the *padang*; the guard house is on the other side and requires a salute every time one passes it. It is particularly pleasant in the evenings. A south-east breeze generally brings that fascinating Eastern smell — that is the only word to describe it. I am brought to a stop many times by this odour, breathe deeply and try to segregate its many ingredients. The poets would just think of all the intoxicating smells they had ever breathed in the East and mix them all together. It is always the same; at least I can't detect any difference. I had heard of and then smelt Africa and anticipated something of a like nature here, but not so. It is entirely different. The Far East has a smell of its own and I have learned to love it. It gets into one's blood and one can now see why anyone having once lived in the tropics always longs for it.

The Dutch bugler has three monkeys, father, mother, and a young one of undetermined sex. The boys gather around to watch their antics, but they have to be tied up as they are very destructive beasts, steal food, etc. We have fifteen Dutch officers and men, naval, 400 Ambons, aside from our 150 officers and 1,000 men. My mess, eight officers, is running fairly smoothly. Petty meanness is always evident, but one learns to expect this now. Little things like: two of them will decide to open a tin of jam, then they forget to tell the others they have gobbled the lot. Or they will keep going strong on it until discovered by the others, at which time it is odds and ends like the bottle of honey from which I got one miserable little spoonful. It was opened at lunch one day and the next day on looking for a share of the balance found it had disappeared.

December 20, 1942 — Another Sunday and erected a drying line near the barbed wire, hear the hymns being sung in a church nearby. Started a large *dhobi* to soak. Had an exercise walk. W/C Coffey got a pasting for smoking on the veranda outside at night. It had always been OK until this incident, but then the little dogs will always find an excuse to give us a pasting. Guess it tickles their fancy to beat up a white man. Rumours, rumours, talk, chatter, inane remarks by the inmates. We shall all go nuts if this continues much longer. My magnifying glass is a god-send. Having sold my lighter for 10 guilders, I purchased this glass, and we get perpetual sun through most of the daylight hours. Even though there is a cloudburst, a half-hour later the sun is streaming through again. Fifty cents for the glass.

December 21, 1942 — We have developed a black market. Senior officers receive twice as much money from Dai Nippon as we do and they have been going around quietly and outbidding for everything in the food line. Our food orders going through the Nipponese show the most amazing things. Officers with plenty of money order their special delicacies for their finer tastes: sides of bacon at prohibitive prices, bottles of ketchup, and expensive sauces; all of this with half the camp starving to death. An officer bought a bottle of port the other day for 13 guilders. He explained he would like to have some port with his dinner for a change. That 13 guilders would have bought 100 kilos of *katjang idjoe*, small green beans about the size of green peas, enough to thicken our watery stew for four days for 1,500 men. I hope he enjoyed his port. An Ambon was selling some food item in one of the officers' rooms. He had asked 6 guilders and they were just getting ready to close the deal at 5 guilders when an orderly from a certain W/C's room arrived and plunked down 15 guilders. Even the Ambon was embarrassed. He apologized to the others, picked up the 15 guilders, and departed hastily. Every day one can see and smell bacon, potatoes, and onions, etc., frying a few doors away. All of which is supposed to be coming through the Dutch-Nippon black market. It's no wonder our other ranks have little use for their officers. When these same officers are approached for a donation to the hospital food fund, of course, they are destitute, flat broke, and it falls on the junior officers with their miserly 10 guilders a month to keep the thing moving. A week ago my attention was drawn to some *katjang idjoe* beans growing outside our billets, obviously planted by former prisoners. A P/O, formerly a Malayan forestry inspector, recognized them and said that this was the very thing our stews were crying for. All that was required was picking and sorting at the cookhouse. Two men could give the whole camp a tremendous amount of food value just for the taking. I took this information to W/C Welch and suggested a two-man fatigue daily. The only noticeable result to date is the six or eight W/Cs out there daily in the patches gathering up the harvest and cooking it on their charcoal fires in the rear of our billets. This bean is similar to our lentils, or green peas, except that it is thought to have tremendous vitamin content over and above its cousins. When we can get them for the camp mess, they are charged to us at 13 cents per kilo. Tempers beginning to flare in our own mess, petty jealousies, petty scrounging, cliques forming to get more of this or that. The mess next door asked us for oranges, limes, and sugar to make marmalade. We shared with them but have not received any of the marmalade.

December 22, 1942 — Two bullock carts full of food arrived about noon; this is a Dutch officer's order and there are only nine of them left here. None of our orders have come through as yet. The Dutch gave us half their order — we are 123 officers and 1,000 men. Then, having a surplus, they sold their balance at a premium. It went like hotcakes. Those nearest to their rooms with the most money got the lion's share. Some rooms grabbed 25 guilders' worth while others got none. We managed 5 guilders' worth — a tin of bully, four jars of peanut butter, two kilos of butter, and a tin of sardines. The fruit issue reached us at noon today as it does about every fourth day — two bananas or a piece of papaya. Blitz on hair on *tenko* parade, eight men and twenty-five officers were hauled out. The English-speaking Nip said five days ago 'it is policy to cut your hair like Nippon *Sama sama*.' Some of our vain people still persist in doing sides and back, leaving some on top for their adornment.

December 23, 1942 — This afternoon more foodstuff arrived. It turned out to be a sort of a Nippon Christmas gift. We got two-thirds [of a pound of food], eleven candies, three small bars of soap. There [was] some clothing for the naked, including shirts, shorts, socks, shoes, underwear, pajamas. Having none of the latter I asked for a suit, but on being informed there were already 250 requests for the seven pair received, I withdrew. Although my shoes are finished, I hardly ever wear them. I've probably been on my feet for a whole day four times in the last eight months. Knowing the men have done all, I dare not ask for shoes. Received a small quantity of peanut oil.

Prisoners lining up to be marched to work — sketch by Andrew van Dijk.

Collection of Jan Krancher

December 24, 1942 — A dull cold day, temperature down to about 85 F. Read a copy of the *Nippon Asia Times* of November 4, 1942, giving the news of the world in English. Judging from the news given in this paper, we have already lost the war and will be prisoners for life. I have quite a store of cigarettes, cigars, and tobacco ahead, enough to take me through any ordinary famine, and although I am broke it is nearing the end of the month and I'll soon receive my princely salary of 10 guilders from our hosts.

Terrific accident in our camp yesterday. The camp commandant was giving himself a solo driving lesson along one side of the *padang*. He knocked down a Dutch officer carrying many dozens of eggs to the hospital (we have to buy these); the Dutch officer was badly cut up and of course the eggs were scrambled precipitately. The Nip proceeded to do everything he shouldn't: threw the steering column hard over and jumped on the accelerator instead of the brake, and keeping it jammed down hard — he was in low gear — ploughed madly into one of the *atap* sleeping quarters, over the veranda, and into the room itself. Bamboo shoring wall and thatched roofs caved in and still he kept going. Men inside, many S.I.Q., others sitting and standing around, were scattered in all directions. Only one officer in this building was seriously hurt — amazing that a dozen of them were not killed considering the nature of the accident, some of the boys having been pushed through several bamboo partitions. It was said, jokingly I guess, that the commandant stepped out of his car and stared vacantly around him waiting for the *kerie* which everyone must give him when he enters a room. Battered, bruised, and sore all over, the group eventually collected its wits, staggered to their feet, and paid their respects. Six hours later, repairs had been affected. Place cleaned out and beds or what was left of them back in position. Remarkable what can be done when there is no red tape. Padres singing hymns in their billets all afternoon and evening. It was announced that we will be able to write six letters a year according to specification. Received an issue of twenty cigarettes and two cigars for Christmas.

December 25, 1942 — I wonder how many feet of snow back home and how many degrees below zero. Our dull day yesterday turned to rain; our roof sheds some of it, so whenever it rains, beds and clothes inside or out get very, very wet. Reveille half-hour early for some special church services. I did not go nor get up until *tenko*. Pap for breakfast. Three more cigars and some coffee issued. Played chess in the evening with Dutch Doctor Ort, had late cocoa with him, milk and sugar, unable to resist and as a result had to get up five times through the night and stagger the 200 yards to the urinal through the mud. Lunch — a loaf of bread as usual, bread in name only. We were able through marvels of abstinence on the part of everyone to augment it with a half-loaf fried in coconut oil, the other half toasted, some fried rice, chilli, and onions, a dash of ketchup, and a small slice of bacon; this went on my fried half, and on my toasted half I had real butter and an abortion called butter. I topped this off with a candy and a cigar. The rice had been saved from the evening before. Held field sports in the afternoon: comic football match, fifty-yard sack race, fifty-yard handicap obstacle race, kicking the football, etc. It was not surprising to find the native entrants carrying off most of the prizes, particularly the events requiring stamina. They all thrive and are getting fat on our diet. Dinner — the usual rice and stew, the stew having a few brown beans added to it. Our orderly came up with a marvellous blancmange, dark and light in colour. A little bit on the tough side in texture; only the orderlies know the ingredients, but it was a nice change, slightly watery to the taste. Topped this off with another cigar. In the evening we were to be shown a movie picture; if they did not show the picture we could have a band concert. We had the concert, marvel of marvels. When I had come back from calling on friends, about 1300 hours, I was told we could write a postcard and they were to be in by 1300 hours, twenty free words and three form sentences. It is now well over a year since I heard from the outside world. Evening orders — all officers under forty-five and physically fit are to work in the outside gardens across the street from the camp. There was an immediate blitz on the medical staff for excuse duty and S.I.Q. chits. Officers received cables from their wives in Australia. They were broadcasted by radio and picked up by the Nippons.

December 27, 1942 — Our padres have all blossomed out into black and white gowns and held many services today. Inspection by Nip colonel in afternoon, nipped in the bud by one of our tropical cloudbursts. Rained for hours and everything got soaked. However, it freshens the atmosphere and washes away all the bugs. Just as hot after as before. Four Dutch civilians arrested today and brought in. They worked on the railways for the Nippons, lovely grub, and is the first time they have been imprisoned. Quite a shock to them. S/L Hopkins is very despondent; at times I've had to be father confessor, priest, brother, as well as friend. He has made me his confidante many a time. He was married three weeks before coming overseas and is afraid his wife will not remain true to him. This thought has become a complex to him and if he doesn't look out he will go bats. Nothing that I can say has any effect.[13]

---

13   S/L Desmond Hopkins, R.A.F.V.R., died September 3, 1944, in the prison camp at Haruku.

December 28, 1942 — S/L Aylwin gave me a shirt and S/L Hopkins gave me a pair of shorts.[14] I had been forced to use my tropical green beach pajamas most of the time for a uniform, as the only things I possessed were becoming so threadbare. The second-hand Dutch uniform I got at Malang only lasted about four washings. These officers apparently got tired of seeing me in my Easter rig and, having plenty, shelled out. Second inoculation against bubonic plague. As the result of the first one at Lyceum Camp, three officers and thirty men went to hospital with septic arms. P/O Donaldson, who was laid up for five weeks, swore it wasn't the serums but the needle that fixed him. Now getting plenty of rain daily, easy to keep clean by bathing under the eaves and we don't have to plough through the mud.

December 29, 1942 — Sun shining and did a huge *dhobi* early. Now worn out. Five bullock carts arrived with our first food order. We were checking goods and were sorting until main event over, but the billets had not been finished when we were waved to the shelter of the eaves. Later we were ordered back to billets, a sorry lot. The rain came from every direction above the horizontal in floods. Bed, mattresses, blankets, spare clothing, in fact everything so carefully dried through the day saturated. Our room had four inches of water on the floor.

December 30, 1942 — To further indulge my fad for writing, I have started a novel. God forbid that anyone else should read it, but it furnishes me with plenty of amusement. Paper and pencils are scarce and I had to adopt a microscopic scrawl. On counting I'm finding that I'm getting over 1,000 words on one side of this very page, an ordinary school exercise book.

December 31, 1942 — Got a terrible beating but otherwise uneventful. Didn't get my *keri* out fast enough to suit one of the little yellow rats. Received small items from the order, but the Nips had cancelled all

---

14   S/L Sidney Aylwin was commander of No. 152 Maintenance Unit, R.A.F.

the tinned foods. Our own medicos, with their bellies and billets full of onions, tomatoes, potatoes, etc. from the Dutch orders, cancelled all our Lombok onions, tomatoes, potatoes, etc. because of the danger of dysentery.

January, 1 1943 — What has this year to offer us? Have we been forgotten? We who are about to die, will anyone avenge us or have we been lost in the scuffle.[15] The bodies will not stand up to very much more of this, or if the bodies do, it seems unlikely that the minds will. But away all depressing thoughts. While there's life there's hope. One might have died a sudden death in battle.

January 3, 1943 — All the officers are about ready to chew up the senior medico. Everyone knows that he couldn't diagnose a common cold and now he has ordered the old, halt, lame, feeble, as well as the sick, to work in the gardens outside. S/L Aylwin, fifty-nine years, old soldier of the last war, swears that he will prefer charge as soon as he is free, will even have the matter hashed over in Parliament. This medico has been blamed openly for many of our deaths in the last camp because of his incompetence and inability to organize the medical staff.

January 5, 1943 — The S.M.O. [senior medical officer] declared me fit for work today, thereby flouting the opinions of Dutch surgeons and our own Doctor Forbes, in my opinion the only doctor who is worth his salt among our lot. When the S.M.O. finished his examination and passed his opinion, he apologized quite handsomely, saying that he did not do this vindictively. 'It's enough for me to know that you deem it necessary to make an apology for this opinion,' I [said].

---

15   Wyse is referring to the famous last words of the archetypal Roman gladiator, 'Hail Caesar, we who are about to die, salute you' (*Ave Caesar, morituri te salutamus*).

January 8, 1943 — Working outside this morning. These gardens were started a few weeks ago and are coming along fine. Five huge bed[s] of corn were weeded out yesterday, including the corn. Few know anything at all about gardening. I've been given a list of Nippon words and expressions miles long which we must learn at once.

January 9, 1943 — *Yasume* Day — no working parties and, of course, as the gardens are well started, we were warned to get ready to move. A hasty scramble to eat up all loose ends, as it is impossible to carry half the things I would like.

January 10, 1943 — A day well remembered by me from five years ago: I was accepted into the R.A.F. for general duties. Reveille at 6 a.m., *tenko* at 6:30, breakfast at 7, fall in at 8 with full kit, march off at 9. Wore my Bombay bowler for about fifteen minutes; it had been hanging over my bed space since the last move. Felt something moving inside, flipped it off and [out] dropped a scorpion. Mr. scorpion hit the dirt and I hit him a half-second later with my both feet. Another lad [who] fell in alongside of me had just discovered a centipede in his luggage which measured six or seven inches. We were given one *yasume* on this march of about five miles, weakened bodies, full kit. Our rest came on the banks of the canal. A beautiful Javanese maiden of some fifteen or sixteen years was bathing in the canal when we came abreast. Her clothes were lying on the bank. Our grinning hosts picked up the clothes and hid them. Venus strolled nonchalantly from the brook, looked around for her clothes, and not finding them waited patiently with all the stoical calm of the East for them to appear. Gesticulating, grinning, and chattering Nips to the contrary, the officer's company failed to derive any amusement from the spectacle. We are back in No. 1 Camp Jaarmarkt and we are packed into the *atap* huts shoulder to shoulder.

January 11, 1943 — This morning we were addressed by the Nip's big N.C.O., and it is on this parade that prisoners are made to bow to the rising sun, the Emperor's palace in Tokyo. Many rumours concerning moves among the officers but I incline more towards the erks; they seem to always come up with the right dope. Came on Lawton last night; his is a pathetic case. I gave him some money when leaving Lyceum five weeks ago, but not enough as I was low myself. He looks very bad, is broke, and should not be working but must to gain the 10 cents per day our generous hosts allow. He is practically starved, the rice is not agreeing with him. M.A. at Oxford University, lecturer on philosophy, an AC2. Thank God I was able to cheer him up financially and other ways.

January 12, 1943 — Rained all night. Keeping me awake and making me have to urinate about seven or eight times. Our *baleh-baleh* beds are twenty-foot lengths of slatted bamboo woven together like a basket. If someone moves forty feet away everyone feels the shock. This was urinating under difficulties. The trough running into an open drain is about 300 yards from our door through seas of mud puddles. On arrival back, one towels down as after a shower and repeat. I am messing now with Uncle Aylwin, fifty-nine, a grand old chap. A former artillery major, full of dry wit and Englishisms.

W/C Ross was in charge of the outside working parties. We fell in at 2 p.m. and usually managed to get outside in a half an hour. The Japanese guard changed at 2 o'clock but the old guard refused to go off duty until the spectacle we presented, falling in and passing though the guard, had passed into history. W/C Ross always got the jitters, made an ass of himself and got the officers into such tangles that it was indeed laughable. The cheers and jeers of the Jap guard did not tend to ease the W/C's blood pressure. And here's our morning parade with another of the jittery ones in charge. The troops call him Miss Vines. Vines gets out of bed and tries to fall in the officers about ten minutes too early so as to be in plenty of time. Nobody can get up in the morning without going to the urinal, others would like to get a wash, but Vines tries to grab them to fall in. He eventually gets about half the company fallen in according to size; individuals keep coming. He runs up and down the lines ranting like a lunatic, 'You change with this man, you change with that man,' and as the men have a little intelligence they usually have to move back

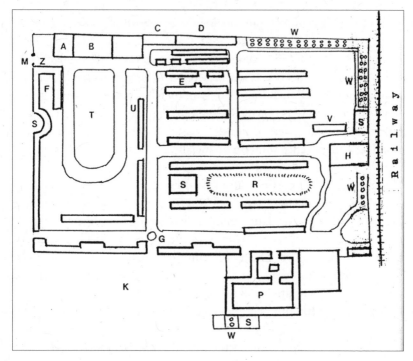

Plan of Jaarmarkt Camp, Soerabaja, at the time of the departure of the drafts.

A	Japanese administration	P	Afd. Pertukangan
B	Main hall	R	8-ft. high mound for patrolling
C	Klompen makers		guards
D	Peanute butter factory	S	Showers
E	Semior English officers	T	Parade Ground
F	Senior cookhous	V	Vogelkooi ("Chicken coops")
G	Camp shop	W	Bore-hole latrines
H	Hospital	U	Camp artists
K	Football ground	Z	Guard-room
M	Main gate		

Collection of Jan Krancher

where they were originally. By why go on? His commands are always wrong and he's scared to death of getting sloshed by the Nips. One morning he unfortunately made the remark: 'You men will drive me crazy.' Sotto voice from the rear: 'You've already reached that stage, Sir.' What fun and games we have. Uncle Aylwin: 'I'm from Poona, by gad, where you don't go out at night. Murdered! That's what you'd be, by gad. And a man is never the same after he's murdered.' Singapore scrotum is now more commonly known as cherry undercards.

January 15, 1943 — The two native soldiers who attempted to escape [and] were caught and tortured for months are here. They were turned loose, but as one of them is off his rocker and the other very vicious, they had to be placed in solitary again. No one allowed to see them. Moving pictures shown last night and half the camp supposed to attend, the other half tonight. As they are Nip propaganda pictures, hardly anyone turned up. Stroll in the evening around the *padang*. Taps and showers doing a roaring trade. A mock band grinding out mournful tunes in the Ambonese billet on string and bamboo instruments with a tin can for a drum. Continuous stream headed east with a bottle in their hands. Erks' quarters, laughter and song, a ukulele strumming, in another a banjo. A Dutchman in an enclosure playing an accordion for a crowd, hundreds standing and seated listening to him and he is good, classical music, marvellous; one could easily picture him seated at the console of a great organ. A cleared room and two Dutchmen putting on a show. A 7' 2" man out for a walk. The whole interrupted at frequent intervals by the '*Kiotski, keri, noware, yasume*' from the pernicious guards. Through the billets every game known to science is being played to help break the monotony. Where boards or cards are required they are manufactured on the spot out of the materials at hand. Those without hobbies indulge in endless bickering, barracking, and quarrelling. There are aimless discussions on the war situation. And, sombre thought — not forgetting the hundreds of S.I.Q. in misery, hunger, and fear of the great unknown, beriberi, dysentery, malaria, tropical ulcers, and no loved ones to succour them in their agony of soul, helpless — hopeless.

January 20, 1943 — The messing combine of S/L Aylwin and yours truly has acquired a kilo of bacon at 3.50 guilders, what a sacrifice, and what a delicious morsel.

January 22, 1943 — I'm thinking of all the cuss words I've ever heard in my life. Somebody stole our bacon! I discovered it first and did not tell my pal. When he did find out he went into a rage, bounced up and down so hard on the *baleh-baleh* that he broke through and landed in the dirt with all his possessions. There he lay for minutes painting the atmosphere blue with all the words I thought of but did not say.

January 31, 1943 — Collected a terrific beating from a half-dozen of our charming hosts and have been laid up for about a week. It all started over a cat, gained momentum through the usual language difficulties, and ended with yours truly out for the count. I had got up to go to the urinals about 3 a.m. one morning. On the way to the door of our billet I came on a cat licking its chops, having just finished a meal from someone's precious store. Shades of our bacon! I picked up the cat and carrying it to the door sent it flying and it landed in a young pond, the result of the evening's downpour. A Nip guard heard the splash and approached to learn the cause. Needless to say, he couldn't understand my English nor me his Japanese, and all Japs have the amazing ability of working themselves into a maniacal temper in very short order. Other guards approached and their sport was on with the above result. Head still a bit woozy but no other ill affects.

Our bread ration was stopped one week ago today. This should clean off many more of the weak ones in short order, if that is what our little yellow friends desire. Had some butter, jam, and peanut butter to go on my bread, but now am putting it into the pap to get rid of it. The butter does not go so well in the pap as it is a little high — gross understatement. The guards have been putting on a display of hate for over a week. They come charging through the camp looking for someone on whom to vent their spleen. The Dutch officers, who were receiving a higher scale of pay than we were, protested on being reduced to our level. We had hoped to be increased to theirs.

February 2, 1943 — Someone ordered a box of toothpicks as a joke. (We haven't seen any meat since the days of the ark.) The Japs missed the humorous angle and delivered the box of toothpicks, 1.50 guilders, which the joker had to pay or else. Eight of our lads have arrived from the old Malang hospital, the others going to C.B.Z. in this town. There are no P.O.W.s left in Malang. Visiting the hospital, a Dutch laddie was telling me about the girl he was engaged to when he passed away. Some of our men were out on a working party the other day shifting freight cars on a siding. Along came the Malang express. The Nip guard flagged the train, detached the engine, and had it do the shifting while the poor prisoners looked on and applauded. The through train was delayed about one hour.

February 8, 1943 — And so passed my first year in Java. How many more? A prisoner in a white man's country knows how long his sentence is to be and one can't but think knowing would be a help.

Self-portrait of a typical prisoner in Java — sketch by Andrew van Dijk. Collection of Jan Krancher

Prisoners doing mandatory calisthenics under the watchful eye of a guard — sketch by Andrew van Dijk. Collection of Jan Krancher

Chapter Four

A Second Year in Java

February 9, 1943 — Many of our erks had a bad time of it on parade today, failing to take their P.T. exercises too seriously. Some of the guards had sneaked up behind in the hope of catching them out. We are being pushed into another billet today to make more room for our valiant wing commanders. The rains continue, worse, if anything. At any moment of the day or night without warning down it comes. Shouts and a mad scramble to get one's clothing off the lines if during the day. Usually what one has gained in one hour of sunshine is lost in a few minutes of flying spray during the storm. Getting plenty of news now, of the Nippon variety. We have two papers coming in daily in quantity. Also one is able to buy fruit and eggs if one has the money. I happen to be suffering at the moment until pay day. The boys are developing serious eye troubles, warning re: scabies. Shaving every fourth or fifth day now as I am out of soap. *Teda apa* — what does it matter. My ailment has been quiescent for some time and I'm holding my fingers crossed. Doctor, inspecting an erk's eyes: 'Read the third line of letters on the chart.' Erk, looking around the room: 'What chart?'

March 4, 1943 — Almost a month since I made an entry in this log, not that there has been nothing of interest to record, but because I am quite worried about my eyes. They are failing and hundreds of the boys are the same. Have had no tobacco since the middle of last month. Foods available have been cancelled repeatedly and the prices have gone up in smoke. I went broke so early last month that I'm trying to be very careful this month, with prices so high. The hell of it is there always seems to be someone who needs my money worse than I do. We had to move into another billet, and although we have a little more space, the place is filthy dirty, dark, and depressing, no air and hotter than the ring-tails. Three of our lads from C.B.Z. came into camp yesterday. They have beriberi, acute cases. The doctors at the hospital sent them back to camp in the hope that there would be more food for them here than they were getting at the hospital. Someone kidded me about rice on my being posted overseas. Little did I dream I'd have to absorb the stuff three times a day, day in and day out for one solid year. With the cutting out of our rice bread, our variety has deteriorated to pap, pap and rice, with a weak and watery stew in the evening. The stew is coloured water with a few grains of carrot or greens of the spinach or leaf variety thrown in. Rarely one gets a surprise in the form of a tiny morsel of meat (buffalo). Have been able to augment once or twice with a few *katjang idjoe* beans.

March 7, 1943 —Went sick this a.m. but it was a Sunday. One is not supposed to go sick on Sundays as it is the doctor's day off, so I shall have to postpone my illness until tomorrow.

March 14, 1943 — There was no pap until 10 a.m. When one is half-starved that makes for a long, long wait. The Nips have been increasing outside working parties considerably and even have the boys out working nights. Three men fell off the dock the other night in the darkness, another injured. Have been S.I.Q. for one week. Wing commanders asked to take over the companies to allow the junior officers more time for other duties, of which there is a multitude. And of course this makes for more crabbing than ever. My buddy is practically blind and I have to do everything for him, prepare his food, roll and light his cigs, etc. He can't even make the urinal now. There were a few cigarettes in on Thursday and mine are gone already. On Monday and Tuesday nights Nip propaganda pictures were shown to us. As no one attended, every individual in the camp was asked to write a thesis on the showing and have it in to the camp office by Wednesday noon. I hope they don't scan too closely the assortment of rubbish that was turned in. To add to my sorrows I now have a wizard attack of prickly heat — scratch-a-like-a-hell-a.

March 21, 1943 — We are getting some marvellous sunrises on the morning *tenko*. We line up with the dawn and while the Nip counts our noses, watch the beautiful changes in colouring through the low hanging clouds. When the count is finished we pay our morning obeisance to the Nippon god in Tokyo. For some time we were able to get away with a 'Good morning, President Roosevelt,' but the Nips became suspicious concerning the loud roar which went up every time we bowed to their god and about a hundred of the boys got beaten up one morning. The United States lies over to the east as well as Japan. Am reading a couple [of] hours a day to my pal, who is almost blind. My eyes do not seem to be any worse and I'm keeping my fingers crossed. As there are few books, I've been reading him some of the junk I've been trying to write. He doesn't seem to notice any difference.

March 28, 1943 — Am down again and can't seem to get up for any length of time. What a head.

April 3, 1943 — Cracky! What fun we have. That delightful headache reported above turned out to be dengue, first cousin of malaria, or more commonly known as five-day fever.[16] It's wizard stuff, I can vouch for that. Carted off to hospital once more. If it had been left to our own doctors I don't think I'd ever have known what I had, had I survived. Twenty-three hours after I was admitted on the authorization of W/C Coffey, who diagnosed my affliction as a common cold and wanted me isolated so that the rest of the boys wouldn't catch it, I had a call from one of our English doctors. I was able to inform him what it really was

---

16   Dengue is a potentially fatal mosquito-born disease.

by that time, as a Dutch doctor friend had recognized me in passing the night before and made an examination. The spots were showing at this time, an indication that the worst of it was over and the fever abating. This disease means violent headaches for days which nothing will abate, and [at] the back of the eyes the ache is abominable. Pain starts creeping through the muscles in the early days and settles in the bones, hence what the Dutch call 'the broke bone stage.' In this stage all the bones in the body ache as though they had been broken. It does not entail a particularly high fever, but one sweats buckets twenty-four hours a day. One suffers a loss of appetite the first day and nothing can tempt one for days on end. One would expect a ravishing thirst with the fever, but even the thought of a drink makes one sick — stomach and head going around in circles. Not one bite of food, not a drop of water passed my lips for four days, and then it was a case of stuff it down and hope for the best. That the food was pap did not help, of course, but not even a nine-course turkey dinner could have stimulated my appetite. One comes out of it completely spent; neither arms nor legs will function for days and the slightest exertion requires about three hours' rest.

April 11, 1943 — Feeling much better and out of hospital. Weight dropped to eighty-five pounds. Rumours of a move for us; some have left already and others are ordered to be ready to move at 8 a.m. tomorrow. The rumours say Bandoeng and that, being in the hills, the climate would be much cooler than down here on the plains; but then again Formosa and Japan are much cooler too. We were shown our third film last night, this one being the Nip blitz on Pearl Harbor and the sinking of *Prince of Wales* and *Repulse*.[17] Once again we were made to write a thesis on the show, but one barrack can get the general idea if only one of its members is curious. These were training pictures, showing how it is done in Japan. All rubbish.

One of our Dutch priests got banged about severely a few days ago for

---

17   The British battleship H.M.S. *Prince of Wales* and battlecruiser H.M.S. *Repulse* were sunk off Malaya by Japanese aircraft on December 10, 1942.

not bowing to a guard when he passed. The priest said he did bow and sticks to it, but his word did not mean anything. Padre Giles held a service the other day, reading it from notes. I can't figure what has stimulated this padre into such strenuous activity. The notes were seized and Giles given three days' solitary. The rains continue, buckets, floods. I pity the poor blokes who are moving; our thatched roof sheds a small percentage of it. Still reading to my pal, Uncle Aylwin. He has a miserable cold now as well. Rats have become a bit of a bind, eating any spare supplies lying about. There are some cats in the camp which have escaped the pot, but they would run a mile from a rat. And it is just about time we were leaving this camp; a few more months and we'd have to raise our billets on stilts or be in the manure. The stink of the place for many months is beyond words, none of the infamous open drains even here. Soon we would have to close the overflowing bog-holes we have dug in all available open places, move our billets over on top of them, and make way for more holes. The Dutch say this town is very low and there is practically no drainage to the sea. However, every move we have made to date has been to something worse than already experienced. W/C (Miss) Vines has been promoted to battalion commander; what a laugh that is, but he is treading on air. Guess he expects to get a Japanese medal.

The cigarette situation is a little easier but one has to guard excess on our mere pittance. I have at least 400 chips in the bank now, I figure; drawing interest, maybe. I shall be a millionaire yet. All Dutch packs, other strong packs, groundsheets, and raincoats were seized in the searches today. The Japs say they need them for their own troops.

One of our Canadian erks in the next billet has constructed a ukulele and can he ever play it. He even goes into the classical numbers, making his instrument sound like a pipe organ. His rendition of the 'Ave Maria' is well worth hearing. 'Cupid' Housley takes over the musical effects after lights out and continues until dawn. His cough should have put him in his grave years ago. It starts on a very high note, comes rapidly down the scale to the very depths, where he gasps for breath, apparently in such agony that one expects to have him expire any moment; suddenly he hits his high note again and commences his run down. This goes on for hours and keeps the whole billet awake, some cursing, others waiting and hoping that someone else will climb out of his net and shy a few heavy objects at him and wake him up. Yes, friend 'Cupid,' through all the fuss and bother, sleeps peacefully on.

April 14, 1943 — Great commotion. First party away on Sunday. The second, including all senior officers and sick, got away last night. A third party is being formed. There have come into this camp 500 Dutch from Batavia, with more expected today; they are joining 1,500 erks, thirty English officers and many Dutch from this camp. This large working party will leave today for parts unknown.[18] This leaves seventy British officers and a few erks.

April 20, 1943 — The big draft was held up somewhere. The remainder of us were told to be ready to move on Saturday morning. Reveille 4:30, breakfast 5, move at 6:30. At 2 a.m. we were awakened and told not to get up at 4:30, that the parade was postponed until 10. Our brilliant administrator would wake us to tell us that we could sleep another hour. At 10 a.m. told that the parade was postponed to 4:30 p.m., move off at 5, then changed again to 2 p.m. This was the hottest day of the year, I believe, and we stood in the hot sun for four hours needlessly. Early evening meal, watery soup and rice, and marched under full kit to the station. I say full kit — I mean that kit which one wanted at the next hell camp in view of what he was able to carry. Many of the men will stagger away from the camps with impossible loads and fall down by the wayside. This usually means a kicking or a rifle butt over the head and is not worth it, as the poor fellow has to stagger to his feet and probably can't pick up anything. Others start off with two packs, one of prime essentials, the other full of things he would really like to have later but which he could do without at a pinch, and the pinch coming en route he can drop the second.

---

18 On April 19, 1943, 2,071 officers and men left Java for the island of Haraku, where they were put to work building an airstrip; 1,021 of them died from starvation, disease, and abuse before the group returned to Java after September 1944.

For this move we have been warned to take only that which we could carry. It is heartbreaking to lose so many knick-knacks one acquires at each camp though, such as shelves, tins, bottles, sometimes beds home-made, etc. After each move it takes many months to get started again on our few comforts. I don't know how many miles it was from the station, but we arrived completely fagged out under the staggering loads. After all, we have been on a deficiency diet for over thirteen months. The train was composed of native carriages, which wouldn't have been used for cattle in any other country. They have straight benches running along the sides and another running through the centre. By the time they had packed about fifty of us with all the baggage into one of these trucks, it was impossible for one to reach, let alone use, the foul-smelling toilet at the far end of the carriage, but it was only a twelve-hour journey. With all the doors and windows locked tight, it is a wonder that only two died.

The situation here is amazing. The prisoners here at this camp, for-merly Dutch barracks, have been living in privacy, good health, and on the very best of food. It is thought that this is a rest camp for the sick, if the Nips recognize such a thing. Near the huge barrack buildings are many private houses used formerly by the Dutch officers and their wives. These houses are now used by the officer P.O.W.s, and I was put in with W/C Bell and eleven others. This place is impossible to describe as yet because I'm still too tired to get around. I caught a cold on that train journey. And it was very cold last night and of course I haven't enough covering for this kind of climate. I am on the floor but I may be able to find a few boards somewhere to make a bed.

April 21, 1943 — We were given a medical examination by a Nip doctor just before leaving Soerabaja. We marched pas[t] at a distance of about ten feet, shirts off, in single file, and at this distance we were judged fit or unfit. The Nip doctors and orderlies wear a gauze mask when they enter our camps. About sixty men were pulled out during the first examina-tion as being unfit but after a hasty consultation they decided that this was far too many sick, so on a second examination they reduced it to twelve. If one has money here they can live quite decently. Our billet has been working wonders. In the early days they bought rabbits and chickens, even ducks, and all have been thriving. I mean reproducing — at the moment they have about twenty rabbits, nine ducks, and five chickens. In our small garden they have been producing tomatoes and sweet potatoes. Ours is a four-roomed house: three sleeping rooms and one common room. In the outbuildings there [are] . . . servants' sleeping quarters, kitchen, native bath, native toilets, and store room. Solid comfort after all we've had. There are about twenty private houses in our street, called English Officers' Street. Dutch Officers' Street is the next one over, and away over on the other side of the camp [is] another row of houses called Banana Ridge. There is a small Officers' Canteen in one of our outbuildings selling chocolate bars, cigarettes, eggs, and fruit, etc. I should be able to put on some weight here — I am down to fifty-two kilos or, I should say, up to that weight. Never since I was a kid of twelve to fourteen years have I weighed so little. Many old friends at this camp, and it is a pleasant change to converse with them. The food is better here than I have ever known it to be as a P.O.W. The Nips gave those officers who are on parties leaving the island all the moneys that have been saved for them in the bank. A friend of mine who was attached to one of these parties received his, but was then taken off the party because of a terrific bashing over the head. He is now a millionaire, in our language, and gave me five bucks. I had acquired a dictionary, English-Dutch, being left behind, and I sold it here the first thing for 1 guilder. The fellow offered me 1.50 so I don't think he was gypped. All of which is a big help, as I was broke two weeks before pay day and here we can buy food. At last we have an English camp commander who has the courage of his convictions, who recognizes the fact that any man has to have food to live even though he does not wear officer's tabs. Here the C.O. asks for three guilders per month from each officer as a contribution towards the common mess pot. You wouldn't believe the amount of beefing this has caused among the new arrivals; some of them actually have refused to make this contribution. We also have a separate messing fund in our billet which takes another 4.50 per month, all of which goes into the belly, leaving 2.50 per to go into the lungs. I eat two duck eggs and two bananas a day plus the Nip ration in an effort to put on some weight. Pennies are very precious and are now being spent with extreme caution. Our billet contains some of its original furniture, garden tools, dishes, etc. No beds, of course, are allowed, and a baseball diamond and basketball court [have] been laid out on the *padang*. The latter encroaches more than somewhat on the former in the left field area, to say nothing of the blacksmith shop in right field, but they have been having lots of fun in spite of a few obstacles. There is a league of sorts in operation. Have a rotten cold and suffering many headaches. The whole camp is surrounded by a seven-foot *atap* wall, plus barbed wire inside and out, but from our windows and high spots in the camp one can view the hills and mountains in the distance and near at hand, in some instances, flowers, shrubs, trees in tropical splendour.

April 25, 1943 — Easter Sunday. On this eventful day our mess put on a marvellous dinner for which we had been saving for some time. Roast beef, roast potatoes, spinach, and gravy; bananas and a cream [pie] made from sugar and real butter. It was the finest meal I have eaten in captivity. We have an unspeakable beast in this camp who goes on the prowl during the night and steals all the money he can find. It has been going on for many months. Last night the thief entered our billet and stole 21 guilders from one of our [accounts] officers. He had an impress of 500 guilders in another pocket which was missed. There is little danger for the guilty one, as everybody has to get up many times through the night to pay a visit and the boys get used to having people wandering around the rooms during the night. Money means food and lack of food means slow starvation on the Nip rations; therefore a thief under these circumstances is an unspeakable bounder and deserves to be strung up. The Nips offered to aid us in putting a stop to this practice by cutting off the hands of those caught.

May 2, 1943 — Heard last night that Sergeant Pilot James, an old friend of mine and a Canadian, had died last June or July in this camp.[19] Dysentery had pulled him down to such a degree that he was unable to stand a very minor operation. He had been out on the beaches in an escape plan for many months after the Dutch capitulated and was one of the very last to give himself up to the little yellow —. S/L Jardine, Canadian, my C.O. here, has been pestering me for articles for the camp paper, published weekly.[20] Ground out two very short, short stories on baseball and now hope for a respite. Twelve men is rather a lot for our twenty-by-twenty-foot four-roomed house, but with windows and doors open twenty-four hours per there is little thought of congestion. And one can spend hours puttering around the garden, cleaning, trimming, planting, etc.

May 9, 1943 — A practice for a Dutch play was dispersed as being unauthorized. The English had put on 'In Town Tonight' last week and it was very good, all things considered. It seems as though the guards have been ordered to stir us up a bit. Dutch officers bashed up on parade. I was umpiring a baseball game on Friday evening when the guards appeared with clubs and bayonets and dispersed the spectators. Shaken to the core, I continued to call 'em as I saw them and funnily enough the game was allowed to go on. Then on Saturday a Nip drill was ordered for all officers both Dutch and English in the camp. The Nip *gunso* [sergeant] took the parade with drawn sword, many heads came in contact with the flat of it. There came a torrential downpour soon after it started

---

19 W/O1 William James, R.C.A.F., of Bowen Island, British Columbia, died July 21, 1942. James was stricken with malaria and amoebic dysentery but what actually killed him, according to Australian doctor Edward 'Weary' Dunlop, was Dutch surgeons' botching an operation on a gangrenous bowel.

20 Alex Jardine of Vancouver joined the R.A.F. in 1937, transferred to the R.C.A.F. while a P.O.W. in 1944, and retired in 1965. In the early days of captivity, this newspaper, *Mark Time*, appeared daily, printed on paper left over from the Dutch garrison and tacked up on a wall. Later issues were printed on Japanese toilet paper.

and 500 or so odd officers and one Nip sergeant got soaked to the hide before they could reach shelter. The parade, one gathered, was a drill using Nip army commands; that's only a guess of course as it was impossible to gather what was really wanted from the shrill shrieks of the maniac in charge.

A grand sing-song at the English canteen in the evening. Our mess bought a hen, cockerel, and four chicks from an Australian doctor. All Aussies have been ordered to be ready to move on [a] moment's notice. We were able to acquire quite reasonably what this fellow's mess was unable to stuff down at the last minute. It's an ill wind! I've put on two kilos already. If we get an order to move now, we shall be unable to eat our livestock in anything under three days — a very unhealthy situation. Have been given a quantity of bumf, for educational purposes is the official explanation. Now I shall be able to get on with more writing. One has to hide every scrap of writing very carefully whenever one leaves the house or whenever a guard steps inside the door. Needless to say they would not take too kindly to some of this stuff. Unfortunately my last pencil is down to one-half inch stuck into the end of a small piece of bamboo for a handle.

May 23, 1943 — Umpiring a great many of the baseball games. No one knows the rules and I suppose I shall have to concoct a set for them. Played in a scratch game yesterday. And I've been asked to umpire one of the big games tomorrow night, [Dutch Air Force] versus R.A.F. All our literature was picked up here on arrival. Many of the lads carried books, yours truly included, but mine were overlooked in the search. Now everybody wants them and I've been using them for study purposes. I believe the books will be released to us in time, as one of the chaps in our billet is helping the Nips to censor them. He is Big Jim King, tall, freckled Scot, former plantation manager in Malaya and a very fine chap. He has handled many thousands of coolies in his many years in the tropics. Since becoming a P.O.W., having associated for many years with coolies and called them everything from soup to nuts, lowest form of mankind, etc., he has now for the first time in his life come in contact with a real cross-section of the English gentlemen: R.A.F., Navy, and Army officers. After the war he reckons he must go back to Malaya and make his apologies to about 20,000 coolies for all the things he called them in the past. He has found out that they are the human beings and not his fellow Englishmen. They are clean-living, happy, companionable, honest, and all those things connected with human decency. It is the Englishman who is the unmentionable so-and-so. We are compelled to do a Nip P.T. drill now which comes over the radio, along with millions of Burmese, Siamese, Chinese, Ambonese, [Filipinos], etc., a part of the Greater Prosperity in Asia Movement.[21] It is interesting to know that when one raises an arm here, millions of others all over the East are doing the same thing, to the glory of Japan and at the point of the bayonet.

May 30, 1943 — Organized walks have commenced, only one-fiftieth at a time.

June 5, 1943 — Senior officers arrived yesterday from Chimaije in the rain. Many old friends among them, including Doctor MacCarthy, Uncle Aylwin, my blind pal, Tiny Mason, etc. Mason was on a hospital train out of Soerabaja and says it was a nightmare. He never expected to last the journey, which lasted thirty hours over a roundabout route. He was placed with others on stretchers, windows closed and door locked, no water, one loaf of bread for the trip. Doctor MacCarthy on the same train predicted that he would not last. However, only two died on the run and one since, as a result. One of the dead cooked in the car with others for fourteen hours and the stench would knock you down. Doctor Mac was blitzed on arrival for remonstrating with a guard, who insisted a hopeless cripple on a stretcher get up and walk. We now have many heart cases to add to our general inflictions.

Many Ambons and Menadonese [natives of Menado, northwest Celebes] are joining the Nip Army; they must like Nip methods better

---

21   Its correct name was the Greater East Asia Co-Prosperity Sphere. It has been argued that P.O.W.s deliberately misused the term to annoy the Japanese.

than the Dutch. Read Goebbels's speech of last February in the Nippon rag and from this speech one would gather that Germany was already finished. He spoke of the crushing setback to his armies and exhorted the people back home to take heart and put forth greater efforts. Quite an amazing speech.

Doctor Mac is the only officer here who came out on the *Warwick Castle* with me. There are many [other ranks] who keep speaking to me from time to time. Kane, a former transport officer, who just sold his watch to a Nip and who has taken a shine to me apparently on my refusal to borrow, has bought me a sweater, 1.50 guilders. It gets mighty cold here at night and early in the mornings and I have practically nothing to wear. He bought four to five Gillette blades from me which I have been hoarding for 2 guilders. As blades are now selling for a dollar each I don't think I can be accused of doing one of my fellow prisoners. And I now can buy some extra food for a time. If one had 100 guilders one could live like a king for a year.

June 6, 1943 — And strangely enough very much like a spring day back home. I am homesick, feel like going on my famous twenty-five mile hikes through the woods. Paper is very scarce. Any kind of scrap that can be picked up is used for writing or rolling cigarettes. Nothing is wasted here nor will I ever waste anything as I live. One of our rabbits died this morning. My expert medical advice — a kink in the bladder. Kane, next to me, is an insufferable snorer. All that has been ever said on this subject could be rolled up and attributed to him.

June 13, 1943 — On Tuesday broke the third finger on my right hand playing baseball. Had to go to backstopping as no one can hold any kind of a pitch. We've constructed a mask but that's all the catcher has in the line of protection. It takes months for anything to heal under these conditions. I have been warned for work in the weaving sheds starting Thursday. Had a bad spell and was down for several days but must be fit for Thursday, else I shall be accused of trying to scrounge out of a job and will probably have to do it later anyway. We have so many habitual scroungers about that I do not like to lay off on account of sickness, for sure as guns I'd be placed in that category.

June 20, 1943 — A week of ruddy hard work, interspersed with periods of acute misery, absolutely worn to a frazzle in the evenings and scarcely able to drag myself off home to a *chari* [bed]. I have 450 men at the sheds, one half of them unspeakable curs who will take every advantage of a British officer and slink like dogs from a Nip guard. Mad Harry, as we call him, in charge and there are various N.C.O.s. Every time Mad sees me he wants to shake hands and he gave me a pat on the back after the inspection. And again, for some unknown reason, there was a huge increase in production during my tenure in office; I say, my, I had six junior officers as well. There was a 200 gram a day per man average increase in the turnout of rope for Dai Nippon and a new high record for bobbins each day for two weeks, 200 to 205. Even the men are happy about this increase and many of them have asked me if I wouldn't stay on permanently. Quite a change from when I started and of course there is a reason, for none of them have had their pants kicked or their heads smashed during two weeks. I collected a few odds and ends on their behalf in the first few days and I collected a few individuals among them and told them in the good old-fashion[ed] Canadian way what I thought of them. I seemed to have gained their respect. The Nips are making heavy burlap sacks out of the rope the boys are spinning. Naturally all our boys are new to spinning and their quota per man per day is 400 grams; the native women outside can do 1,000 per day. Called to make a full report to W/C Nichols, our camp commander. He is responsible for the splendid organization of this camp and I congratulated him on his good work.

A streak [of] luck yesterday. My Nip hosts at the weaving sheds insisted I take half a day off and go on one of the organized walks. I was so ill and tired at noon that I hardly dared risk it but was certainly glad I went, as the Nips now say there will be no more. We can blame this on the Dutch. The march turned into comedy, the long columns of prisoners then on all sides running, gesturing, and shouting [at] Dutch women, girls, dusky maidens, and children. We of course had been ordered to remain silent under any circumstances. But the Dutch, with many relatives and friends around them, more than stepped out of the crease. As a result they have ruined these marches for thousands of their fellow prisoners. The highlight of the day came miles out in the country during a *yasume*. The Nips allowed a little girl carrying a baby through the lines. The call went around for a Dutch captain to come and see his child. Amazement, doubt, consternation, and everything else registered on his face when told he was a father. At first he claimed to the contrary, much to the amusement of his friends. We've been sixteen months in a prison camp. To my inexpert eyes the baby did appear to be six or eight months and would just come under the wire. Overheard from a charming dark-brown maiden of sixteen or seventeen: 'I brought my food for the English.' Why? — 'Because they have nothing. The Dutch have everything. They are pigs.' Many Germans in evidence around the city, two white girls on horseback, many Nipponese civilians, and we marched through magnificent country. All the females had brought food, cigarettes, and candy for the prisoners and we were allowed to accept these during the rest period through the gracious benevolence of the Japanese Army.

June 24, 1943 — A welcome day in two ways — pay day and my release from the sweat shop. Funnily it was a very successful two weeks and I suppose I should not complain. Oh, yes. Mad Harry is a sadist, an absolute maniac; that is why the men were so glad to have a little peace. He delights in punishing prisoners, torture amuses him.

June 27, 1943 — Many weeks into the dry season now but still getting daily downpours. I was umpiring a baseball fixture Friday night. We had finished one and a half innings when some guards came out and started kicking a football around the diamond. They offered to allow the boys to get the ball for them for exercise. There is a real football pitch just outside the camp gate but that wouldn't bother the prisoners. I haven't been getting enough sleep because of the king snorer next me. Everything in the room which is movable gets hurled at him during the night; if awakened he snorts once or twice and then starts in again. Every note on the keyboard major and minor gets sorted out during one of these performances. About every five minutes he apparently gasps his dying breath, shudders, shakes, and starts again. Our rooster, the 1 a.m. and 4 a.m. one, finally overstepped the mark. He crowed three times between midnight Saturday night and 7 a.m., thus unwittingly sealing his doom. The bloody thing, although only seven or eight months old, was as tough and stringy as a rail fence.

July 4, 1943 — Twelve in our house made a big celebration of Independence Day, bumped off a cockerel and three rabbits for a wizard stew, reminiscent of the Canadian backwoods. A bridge team had the nerve to challenge me to a session at a banana per hundred. I have to take any partner I can pick up. We won forty-seven bananas the first sitting and another eighteen in a return match, and as this is too far out of proportion for our lowly circumstances I settled for one banana from the chastened ones. Capt. Terluin made me a donation of some wizard paper which I have bound into book form, also a pencil. I've been teaching him English. Now have enough paper to keep on writing for a year or so and only wish to be left along with my hobby. My clothes are falling to pieces; I've been patching so often that I've had to patch over patches many a time, until the cloth just pulls apart at a touch. Underwear, such as it is, is in like shape. I have, or had, two towels; they wouldn't be used for a floor mop back home now, but what can one do. Washing is now a matter of light rinsing and hanging out to dry as is, for one couldn't wring them out without committing them to the scrap heap.

July 18, 1943 — Don't know why I didn't write last week. Had collected many bits of interest and now I have forgotten them. Memory fades as hunger increases. The move has not taken place yet although a party has been segregated and are living in the weaving sheds. Ten days of air-raid practices. It is small consolation here to learn that our troops have landed in Sicily and that Africa has been cleared. Read *Oliver Wiswell* this week. Have just waited ten months to get it in my turn and it is the only thing

I have read in six months.[22] Have been trying to write a novel and am thoroughly disgusted with it. There is a tremendous lot of bickering and bad feeling in our mess but it has always been the same. One can only withdraw within oneself and try to be tolerant.

Many [air raid warnings] day and night. Blackout complete to turning out lights makes the evenings a complete bind. W/C Walker bought three ducks and a drake, so he thought, but it was the other way around. After two weeks of close confinement with the three drakes the poor duck keeled over and died. Only then was the awful truth discovered. We had asked for ninety ducks and ten drakes originally and received some[thing] like the reverse of those figures from the Chinamen outside, and there is apparently no redress. We have over 300 now but it has been a struggle, with many dying of beriberi. No matter how many died the keepers have had to show the exact figures daily to Donald Duck, name applied to the little waddling Nip in charge on the books. They allow a one percent shrinkage only and if eight pass out overnight only three can be shown regardless. We set twelve eggs sometime ago, later reducing it to nine, then seven, and five, and eventually got out two chicks, one of which we had to bump off because of a deformity. Eleven good eggs gone up the spout.

July 23, 1943 — Feeling a little better than at any time during my confinement. Time passes much more rapidly now than at first, due no doubt to my being submerged in my hobby most of the waking hours. Today was a day of surprises. In the morning at eleven I counted up my remaining finances for the month, a total of 15 cents, and decided on a grand splash in the form of a celebration of my birthday at our canteen — in other words, coffee and cakes. W/C Bell was leaning on the canteen bar as I entered and I asked him if he was having coffee. He made a suggestive

---

22 The bestselling novel *Oliver Wiswell*, by Kenneth Roberts, is the story of a student who sides with the British during the American Revolution. Major-General Walter Short admitted to the enquiry into the Pearl Harbor debacle that, before assuming command in Hawaii in February 1941, he hadn't read the briefing papers left for him by his predecessor but instead had passed the time reading *Oliver Wiswell*.

shrug and informed me that he was broke. So I showed him my 15 cents, told him of my intended binge, and asked him to join me. We went into spasms of laughter when the barman produced two cups of coffee, a small anaemic-looking biscuit, and a knife to split it with. I think that was the tip off. Bell is in our small mess and when I was called to supper at 6 p.m. the first thing that caught my eye was a menu down at my regular place with a very striking though not too favourable caricature of yours respectively, rear view, in a ridiculous umpiring pose shouting my now famous 'Foul Ball'; underneath was 'Happy Birthday Buck.' Here's the menu for this grand spread: wine — Bucktouche Cocktail (Sugden 1943), clear soup, bearspaw pie (buffalo meat), roast potatoes, cabbage, *katjang idjoe* beans, onion sauce, Wigwam salad, coffee, and flapjacks. The boys had scoured the camp to find the ingredients for this magnificent feast and all on my behalf. Incidentally the wine was a concoction produced by our batmen, a fermentation of *pesang* and papaya. The bottle was tin-foiled around the neck and wrapped — printed on the wrapping — Bucktouche Special, Der Rot Plume, 1066. I have collected many nicknames while in service; out here — bearspaw, foul ball, tiger, Bucktouche, the latter contracted to 'Buck' and the most prominent. It came from a yarn I spun about our old Moncton and Buctouche Railway to the boys many months ago. I have never seen such a spread or witnessed such a demonstration since becoming a P.O.W., and I must say I felt considerably bucked. I am told that the boys searched the camp over for white aprons and caps to go with the service, but were unable to click. The pie was suitably inscribed with greetings, dear knows how, and there were three quarts of the Sugden 1943 — Sugden being the name of the batman who made the stuff. We topped off the meal with cigars. There was a grand climax to the party just after we had settled in bed for the night in the form of an earthquake. All had retired by three minutes to midnight when we felt the first shock. I was tossed around in my bed like a cork on the ocean and my first lightning thought was that I had imbibed too freely of that Bucktouche Cocktail.

August 1, 1943 — The minor shock, as I thought, proved to be a major catastrophe for several towns not far from here on the south coast. The epicentre of the quake was only seventy-five kilometres off the centre of the south coast of Java and, as the crow flies and without the aid of maps, I reckon about 200 kilometres or 120 miles from Bandoeng, our present home. According to the *Nippon News* broadcasts from Batavia, renamed Djakarta by the Nips, Mussolini has abdicated, a new cabinet formed in Italy, the invasion of Sicily by American, Canadian, and English troops, Africa cleared. Apparently these attacks are progressing favourably, precipitating a crisis in Musso's government. The whole world, from the Nip point of view, is crying out in horror over the bombing of Rome and of course they know nothing about the German methods used in bombing the English towns [of] London, Coventry, Bristol, Plymouth. Our Menado friend of Lyceum Camp fame essayed another escape last week, apparently having forgotten his nine months of torture for the last effort. He is now being given a similar dose here of torture. The Nippon commandant, on being approached by our officers to shoot the man and put him out of his misery, claimed that this fellow is a bad man and must be punished before he is shot. More recently they have come to the conclusion that the man is screwy and knew not what he was doing; that seems the probable solution and we all felt that he must be crazy after what he went through. Soerabaja, our last stopping place, has been bombed by American planes, the first indication that the war might be approaching this area. The parole walks, which have been stopped and started several times, were reintroduced yesterday and W/C Bell got out for a hike in place of an officer who was unable to walk because of diseased feet. Dogs got into the rabbit hunches next door and killed three. They have tried our yard at night and we have some hefty clubs waiting for them when they come through our bottleneck entrance. These dogs belong to the Nip guards and it is doubtful if we could get them into the stew pots without attraction. One of our fellows stepped on a baby rabbit the other day and we only discovered it today. It had a broken leg and must have suffered.

Wine

BUCKTOUCHE
COCKTAIL

(SUGDEN - 1943)

Menu

Clear Soup

BEARSPAW PIE
Roast Potatoes, Cabbage
Kajang Idjoe
Onion Sauce

WIGWAM SALAD

COFFEE AND FLAPJACK

FOUL BALL!

HAPPY BIRTHDAY....
BUCK

Souvenirs of the dinner
held to celebrate Robert
Wyse's forty-fourth
birthday. The family of R.N. Wyse

The baseball games are discouraging, with the Dutch teams trimming all comers unmercifully. We are faced with the problem of making players from cricketers, footballers, etc., Englishmen who [have] never seen the game. Caught for the British officers last night and got trimmed about twenty-five to five, yours respectfully scoring three of our five runs and making at least fifteen of the put-outs from behind the plate. Only a baseballer knows what that means when it is known that there were no strike-outs. The best of the Yankee and Canadian players have been posted away to the slave labour gangs, those remaining being either too sick to play or [having] never played the game in their youth. It's funny the ruddy English don't make a cricket pitch; every male of the species plays that game, but no, they will play baseball, want to learn the American pastime. One of the Jap guards told me recently that baseball had been banned in Japan because of the game's American origin.

Our chicken ranch is back to the magnificent production of three eggs per day after a broody spell. The poor darlings have the perpetual look of a drowned rat or a rung-out dishcloth. They too are suffering the pangs of hunger as they only get what scraps we don't eat aside from grass and snails we can find around the camp. A beriberi hen, having no feathers to speak of, [is] a woeful-looking object. My socks are done, finished, too rotten to mend. Cotton from my canvas groundsheet has held them together for some months. My lone towel is in shreds and will now have to become a dishcloth. At the moment I am taking my shower in the afternoons so that I can dry in the sun. Also, the baseball has ruined my only shoes, and of course they were in the semi-state of ruin before baseball. Now I must quit or play in bare feet and there are many small stones on that diamond. Kane has reached new heights in nocturnal embellishments in spite of two operations to open the passage. He is a married man, God help him.

I am keeping a rigid budget scheme this month in order to keep myself solvent. Eight cents a day covers it except for the last day. A small cake of soap just before leaving Soerabaja lasted me until one week [ago]. I can't replace it as it has gone up to 35 cents for a 5 cent bar. Pencils are now 25 cents for an ordinary 1-center and I shall have to splash soon, as I am down to a dozen butts which I use right down to the last piece of lead. Paper is in good state at present through gifts from friends. My hands are an awful mess from beriberi. My broken finger is coming along, although slightly bent where there shouldn't be a bend. We had another banana special at bridge last night; it's got to be quite a joke and I've won something like 300 bananas in theory. One of these days they'll trim me and I suppose they'll expect to be paid in bananas.

The Dutch and English draft having finally moved off, we have had them replaced with Ambonese and Chinese troops. Bedbugs continue to flourish and I can score many kills daily. It is peculiar how little such things bother me now. I only look for the ruddy things from force of habit and not from any inconvenience they cause me. To date we have been fortunate in keeping clear of lice. Mosquitoes are not such a nuisance here in the hills; the Dutch say they are not the malaria-carrying type. Possibility of an operation for me right here in Bandoeng.

August 15, 1943 — Pulled my left shoulder on a peg to second about a week ago. Oh, calamity! Why do I try to play that game while in this condition? Haven't had a sleep for a week. And training this team of nitwits is such a hopeless task that I think I'll drop it anyway. Have had a series of punishment parades inflicted upon us. No one seems to know why except the Japs. Perhaps it's a form of retaliation for American victories. Another severe earthquake shock somewhere on the island, don't know results yet. Have had my cheap watch cleaned and repaired with the view of trying to raise a few guilders. My prized fountain pen will then be my only remaining gadget of any intrinsic value.

August 22, 1943 — Got 5 guilders for my Parker fountain pen last Thursday and shall eat well for a short time. On Friday all officers signed for an increase in pay to 25 guilders per month. We can only wait and see what happens. The Nips will probably feel highly insulted and start another blitz on the whole camp. Our C.O. is really doing his best for all the sick and afflicted. His camp fund buys food for the camp kitchens, which is equally divided throughout. He wants an increase in pay, naturally, to obtain more food for the unfortunates. Of course nothing will come of it, but in the event that it does I withdrew my watch from the canteen sales department. The 3 guilders will do me well for about two months in an environment where one treats cents as a four-year-[old] lad would at a candy counter.

Was inveigled into catching in a fixture last night — England versus Holland — and am a mass of aches and bruises. Lost thirteen-seven but have found a good working combination for the infield which will steadily improve I hope. Some of our professional actors and script writers organized a review which has been running all week and it is exceptionally good. We lost many of the actors as well as baseballers during the move and it has taken some time for others to take over and get things moving.

September 6, 1943 — On Tuesday received 25 guilders from Dai Nippon at the *Kempetai* [Japanese military police]. The Nip commander made a speech of explanation. 'It is the policy of Nippon to improve conditions for prisoners and owing to strict Army control of Java, the cost of board, lodging, and amenities can now be reduced from 60 to 20 guilders per month.' According to this I shall be getting more money and banking more by 15 guilders per month. I must now have about 600 guilders in a bank somewhere.

Had an air-raid warning from midnight until 6 a.m. last week but nothing was heard. Last night through the Nippon news we heard of a three-point landing on Italy by English troops from 100 transports. '*Ding-ting, banas banas*,' the cry of the street vendor passing my window. Another prisoner who makes candy to try to earn a few pennies . . . comes many times a day calling out in a high musical voice. The C.O.'s big blitz on our new pay does not start until next month and I have a surplus to start on which should last me for months. R— has a surplus too which he neither expected nor wanted. A Nip guard spotted his watch one night, offered 60, then 100 guilders for it and took it after many gestures and shouts, offering to give R— a sound bashing if he refused to sell, and in which [case] the watch would have gone for a

Burton for nothing. The guard made him promise as a Christian not to report the matter to the *Kempetai* on threat of another beating. One of our newcomers, a Eurasian, was beaten up most distressingly in the weaving shed yesterday, then taken to the office and ordered not to complain to the *Kempetai* about his treatment. He had only been on weaving for a few days and could not do it to suit Mad Harry, my old friend. Our new cock has gone the way of all flesh. He developed the habit of beating his wings most resoundingly and crowing from about 4 a.m. onward (imbecile). The question then arose as to whether we shouldn't kill off the rest of the chickens with him and put Kane, the king snorer, out there by himself. In view of the fact that the birds were producing, not very much but some, we decided to let the birds live and kill Kane.

September 12, 1943 — *Yasume* Day and Sunday will now be our official rest day. The Nip commandant thinks we should do more exercising for the good of our health, so he has decreed that we construct another outside garden next door. We start tomorrow morning. I predict a move inside of three months, as we've never had a crop from one of these yet. Many letters came in and were distributed during the week. I think this is the second batch in eighteen months. Two officers in our billet received one from England, one dated June 1942 and the other July; there are hundreds more at the *Kempetai* awaiting [the] censor and dear knows there may be one for me. It doesn't matter much really because I've given up expecting one and it [would] probably be fifteen months old in any case. I have addressed two or three letters and about four official cards to Canada but I doubt if any of them were sent away. All letters received were written on spec. And the authors do not know if the addressees are prisoners or stiffs.

September 19, 1943 — As my section of the so-called garden is nothing but huge boulders and the mentioned clay, I am endeavouring to turn it into a rock garden. Yesterday morning a Nippon guard entered our house at 7.30 a.m. Everyone is supposed to arise and make for the parade ground at the instant. Only one man was really up. Needless to say the house arose as one man but there were no cheers. Kicks and blows accelerated the general progress towards the parade grounds which yours truly evaded by having done a nosedive through the window on the first shouted *keri*. Work doesn't agree with me today; my hands are a mass of blisters and every muscle and joint [is] crying out in agony.

The C.O. is apparently justifying his colossal blitz on our pay envelopes starting next month, as there has been a good deal of beefing already from some of our officers. He has nothing to worry about. W/C Nichols has what it takes and most of the fellows realize the position our men are in and we are responsible for them in so far as we are able to help. Coo!

Later. Two pieces of news of tremendous importance to us. Our king snorer is to go into hospital again for a third op on his nose. I don't wish him any hard luck but I hope he never returns to this camp. Secondly, the Nippon commandant, a short time ago, handed to our C.O. a sheath of newspapers, the *Nippon Times*, wherein we learn of the unconditional surrender of the Italian forces to the British armies. Have not seen the papers yet but naturally our joy is confined. In fact many Nip guards have been around to wipe the smiles off our faces.

September 26, 1943 — Paid this a.m. and still have 10 guilders from last month. Wizard! Our shovel brigade, the officers outside garden party, stood three hours in the hot sun and had sticks and stones hurled at them from the rear by the Japs. If anyone turned around or attempted to duck he received special attention. Someone in the ranks had chuckled at something told by a friend and of course we are not allowed to be happy while the Nippon Army is fighting and dying for humanity. Quite a number of our officers will be *hors de combat* for some time. The Nips pulled a good one on parade the other morning. We line up and wait for a Nip guard to come and count us. On this day nothing happened for an hour, at which time there came a runner from the camp office with these orders: anyone having anything in the nature of camp duties or anyone having anything to do could leave forthwith. Thirty-three officers and dear knows how many men remain standing on the parade ground until late in the afternoon. Some people were born dumb and will never grow up. Yours truly was one of the first to smell a rat and was one of the first to leave in the morning. Hundreds of the victims fainted, not once but many times. Early in the afternoon I slipped up behind the workshops, signalled to W/C Bell, and slipped into his place relieving him. He went to billets and ate his rice and rested for an hour but then returned to take over.

My socks and towels are finished but I have to keep using the shreds, with light cotton socks costing 4 guilders, anaemic-looking towels 12 guilders. One of our lads offered to rebuild my shoes for 12 cents but I prefer to buy the extra banana. My feet are toughened to the place where they will take anything now. Have been demonstrating to the British and Dutch baseball teams the inadvisability of their attempting to steal second base with yours truly catching and I've got a good cricketer playing second base. Ordinarily, [when] these people reach first base they run hog wild but with lack of timing and wild throws. They have even been stealing third. They are quite amazed to find the ball arriving there ten or fifteen feet ahead of them.

Little news of moment coming to us through the Nippon press. We have one English and Dutch [radio] set functioning all the time, which the Japs have not found as yet. The penalty is death. We know the Germans are withdrawing rapidly on all fronts.

October 3, 1943 — The rainy season is nearly here and we have had a few good ones to start with and believe me they have worked wonders for us, in this country of open drains rain provides the only sewage system. Our Shit Creek, as it is called, had been dry for many weeks, getting a light flush out in the evening only. This is the sole removal system for the camp and, naturally, with our restricted quarters for the thousands, things pile up in monumental fashion to await a few drops of water. Up Shit Creek is a reality here. That is the official designation given the garden path running from our place to Canteen Street because of the huge sewer which parallels it. Perhaps some of our street and place names would be of interest. We have the Menado Camp, Weaving Sheds, *Kempetai*, Dutch Street, Officer Street, The Arch of Sighs (over Shit Creek), Firth Bridge, Duck Pond, Meatery, Piggery, *Padang*, Tania Bar

(Dutch), Allied Canteen (British), Radio City (gymnasium used for play productions), Pig Row, Banana Ridge, Coffee Bar, and Café (British).

October 19, 1943 — Have been horizontal for about ten days. A draft of 150 men and officers leaving Tuesday. What money they have is being turned into Nippon currency. The rainy season has arrived with a vengeance, day after day of it. Our gardens have been flooded but we must go out and fiddle about in the muck. Everyone must be making aimless pokes at the soil when the guards go through or else. One gets damp and cold and the sun is our only radiator. My clothes are in a frightful mess, everything falling to pieces, and yet I shall have to make them last for a year or more for there is nothing obtainable in the way of cloth. Remaining in this camp are many English officers and none but unfit [other ranks] — about 250 of them.

October 24, 1943 — Rained like the dickens all week, generally started in the afternoon and finishing sometime during the night. The Nips are working a new gag on us now. We were out six days last week on the garden party, but only on one of those days would the Nips give us tools to work with. We are supposed to find sticks and poles etc. and work on happily with them. Anything to show the superiority of the Nippon race over the whites. I'm off my grub, stomach, wizard headaches, and sore eyes. It couldn't be slow starvation because the Nips are so generous with their food. Don't we get our rice ration every day? Last week the Nips sent in fifty 200 lb. bags of rice to the piggery, which their cooks had condemned as unfit for human consumption. One of our officers chanced to see some of this rice through a torn bag, made a closer examination of other bags, whereupon he reported to the C.O. That night, with some of our chaps watching out for the guard, an organized party of British removed fifty of the condemned bags from the piggery and put them in our kitchen store, replacing them at the piggery with fifty bags of the festering rot they give us for rice. It can be said that they give us plenty of meat, for the rice we receive is alive with animal matter. Properly cooked these small animals blend well with the rice.

The Dutch have just finished playing a magnificent review. It went for two solid weeks to packed houses. The costumes were beyond description, wherever the material came from, and the boys playing the girls' parts would pass for lovelies anywhere. I saw it twice and was much taken with the leading lady's voice as well as her charm. She, or he, has a lilting soprano voice which would be well received in any theatre in the world. They put on a Harlem scene which impressed me, all Negroes, and 'Where Is Minnie,' a white girl who did the jitterbug to perfection, accompanied by a small Negro orchestra of swingsters. I have never slept so soundly in twenty-five years as I have since Kane, the world's best snorer, went to hospital.

October 31, 1943 — Have an attack of squitters or dysentery, can't tell which yet. What is called a Sumatra out here struck on Thursday afternoon (hurricane or tornado). Straight walls of water are seen approaching. About half the fences around our camp were either damaged or blown away. Trees, branches, *atap* huts, everything loose departed hence and we received an assortment of debris from the next county.

November 3, 1943 — A big Nippon holiday and a day off for us thanks to the generous Nippon Army. The baseball diamond worked overtime. Our first game of the new league and the slugs trimmed nine to two. Have received a medical, a postcard, and our specimen sheets, so it looks like we are moving.

November 21, 1943 — There have been two or three air raids announced on Soerabaja and we had an alert lasting about three hours. We are compelled to do fire watching during alerts and respond to the Nippon guards in charge in Nippon '*Foo shin gin, ego ari ma sen*' (phonic spelling, meaning, I think — house man, nothing to report). The slave gang working in the outside gardens has been given one hell of a time. The rains have turned the whole area into a quagmire, but we must continue to poke at it aimlessly under the watchful eye of Dai Nippon. One can only stick a shovel into the muck, pull it out, and then scrape it off with a stick. Having extracted a mess of this glue from A and worked it in the general direction of B, one then goes into reverse and transfers it from B back to A; of course the whole business was designed to further humiliate the white officers.

We executed six chickens for a special dinner for the going-away lads last night. There was one roast chicken left over from the feast, which we drew for — I was unlucky. The draft left this morning, Monday: 175 men and three officers. They are reputed to be joining a party of Chinese, also 450 Dutch with eight officers for an unknown destination. We are rumoured to be moving the first week in December; where the rumour came from, dear knows, but our other ranks, out on working parties and at times in conversation with the Nip guards, generally come up with the right dope.

Our old friend Mad Harry paraded all the officers this morning who had been working in the gardens the day before. It seems that something is missing from some buildings in the area where the Dutch officers are working. Mad Harry picked the hottest spot he could find for the parade, stood the officers at attention, and waited two hours for someone to confess to the theft. Two cats appeared and our friend gathered them to him where he was lying in the shade. One of them eventually escaped but the other was slowly tortured to death amid mirthful chuckles from this maniacal beast. The cat, with tail cut off, eyes poked out, limbs dislocated, cigarettes burning stuffed up its nose, finally expired after an hour and a half of this when thrown twenty feet into the air to land on the pavement. This gentleman was a former school teacher in Japan. His savageness in punching, booting, and clubbing prisoners about for no reason whatsoever is a byword in this camp.

In this camp [the] Nip commandant allows us extra food — if we can pay for it. And food is the all-predominant factor in this weird existence; that we are treated like a herd of cattle does not seem to matter any more. The Nips have been blitzing all officers for some time. Gunso Hoshino, another maniac, is responsible for this.[23] It is said the guards say openly

---

23 Author Laurens van der Post, who was also imprisoned in this camp, refers to this guard as 'one of the most dreaded of the Japanese warrant officers.'

that he lost his chance for a commission in the Japanese Army because of seventeen varieties of V.D. [about] which he boasts. Our rabbits are in a precarious state, what with the contemplated move; they are too small to kill right now and yet we don't want to have to wolf the lot at the last minute. There was another attempted — this time — suicide last week. The prisoner was still living when cut down and taken to hospital. Have not heard the ultimate result of the attempt. Of the British remaining in this camp, we have about ninety men all invalids or in hospital and about 150 officers. There are many Dutch officers remaining with many sick; no Americans, Chinese, or Australians. According to our news sheets, Nippon propaganda, the position in Italy remains stationary, the Russians are suffering their usual severe repulses, and the Yanks are observing wicked punishment at Bougainville, in the Solomons. When the Yanks raid any part of this island the Nips cut off our gas, used for cooking in the kitchens, even though the raid is 500 miles away. All cigarette lighters have been confiscated; that is all the little yellow bees were able to find. Some of our electricians constructed immersion lighters, taking juice from the power lines. These have now been done away with, accompanied by the usual bashings.

November 28, 1943 — We are [in] the midst of a diphtheria epidemic, several billets quarantined. The situation is still obscure. I have fallen heir to a top part of a kimono, woolly material. Three cheers. I shall cut and sew it into a towel. Worked out a grand scheme of salvage on my last towel, which was in shreds in the middle. I snipped through what remained of the middle and sewed both ends together, this excellent result giving me many more wipes. I shall patent this idea on my return to civilization. It rains, rains, and rains; buckets, tons, rivers, oceans of it. Starts about 2 p.m., pours all day and far into the night. A little sun through the mornings and then bang — down it comes again endlessly, week in and week out. There has been no baseball or P.T. (mixed blessing) for about a month. Across the street from our prison camp there is an army camp of Javanese who have joined the Nip Army. Any part of the day they can be heard singing for our entertainment 'God Save the King' and other songs in English. Their rendition of the 'Star Spangled Banner' is a decided flop. The entertainment ceases and the entertainers scatter like monkeys when a Nip or a Korean guard appears. Theirs is a dog's life, foot slogging all day, drill with wooden rifles, and from my observation, never get a night out, being closely guarded by the Japanese. No doubt they will be glad to see the coming of the Yanks or the British. There are many rumours about moving. It will probably be to Japan this time, and I shudder to think of that climate in my few remaining rags. Our small loaf of bread (homemade) has improved somewhat in the hands of the Dutch cooks. This stuff is made from a mixture of tapioca and rice flour, all we are allowed, and the result is an unmentionable chunk of dark-brown glue with the strength of shoe leather and the elasticity of an India rubber ball. Half a loaf, about two-and-half-inches square, and a cup of tea, no milk, no sugar. That blooming flour is a part of our rice ration and has to be eaten some way. We've tried it boiled in water and the result does not, repeat not, compare favourably with Cream of Wheat. Our camp subscription was reduced to 11 guilders this month as there are few men left. This gives me a small surplus of cash which eventually will find its way into my belly.

December 1, 1943 — *Yasume* Day. A blitz is being made on all writing. There are a few Nips who can read English and they regard all writing as being something of a subversive nature. I'm afraid they wouldn't take kindly to many of the facts and impressions put down in this log, the odd bits and pieces of which I have kept hidden in *atap* walls, thatched roofs, and inside bamboo poles. On too many occasions has some part of this script been stuffed inside a shirt on the sudden descent of a Nip guard. We have been warned that we can carry no writing with us on our next move. I shall prepare a container and a hole in the ground in our garden out back and keep writing as long as I'm able.

December 23, 1943 — Every man in this camp was herded into the compound in the camp next door while the Nips search our quarters today. Before we were allowed to return to billets we were given the closest search of our imprisonment. In the personal search large sums of money were confiscated and the holders given a severe beating. Thousands of dollars in our camp fund was found, also a Dutch fund, which [was] confiscated. Everything in writing, down to a sick in quarters chit, was seized, including all writings, reports, personal papers, etc., and are now burning merrily in front of the *Kempetai*. I experienced many qualms during this search, as a sectioned three-inch bamboo pole leaning against the wall in our garden contained all my writings. The bamboo pole idea came through with flying colours. But I lost every other scrap of paper otherwise. Rather than sweat my life's blood again, this stuff goes into the ground come dusk. The Japs say we have been receiving too much money by the large camp funds found (a grand scheme on the part of our C.O. gone up in smoke); therefore they will cut our pay in future and they insist that we must spend the entire sum of both camp funds, some 30 guilders, before the move, which takes place in two or three days' time. On pointing out that this couldn't possibly be done and the food eaten, the Nips say they will spend it for us. And now this screed goes into a large candy bottle in the hope that someday I shall be able to return and dig it out.

Conclusion

Robert Wyse's diary ends there. He was not the only prisoner to decide that record keeping had become too dangerous. Through the summer of 1943, the Japanese Army regular soldiers guarding the prisoners were replaced by even more brutal Japanese and Korean conscripts, and any illicit activity became riskier than ever. The most famous diarist in the camp, Laurens van der Post, buried his journal of eighteen months in captivity, and others who had done pencil sketches or maintained the camp's accounts also secreted them away. Remarkably, most of these documents survived the war to be reclaimed later. Over the next eighteen months, groups of prisoners would leave Java for the works camps of the Burma-Thailand Railway, the Spice Islands, Formosa (Taiwan), Korea, and Japan, but Wyse was not among them. This fact probably saved his life, for the death rate among the P.O.W.s in Java declined marginally, while it rose dramatically for prisoners in other parts of the Japanese Empire.

When Allied forces arrived at the prison camps of Java in August and September 1945, they found thousands of malnourished prisoners clinging to life. Many were beyond hope, but Robert Wyse, though he weighed less than ninety pounds, was alive. Wyse left Batavia on H.M.T. *Sobieski* in early October 1945, travelling via Colombo, the Suez Canal, Port Said, Malta, and Gibraltar before putting in to Liverpool. He had not had a

Robert Wyse and Laura (Teakles) Wyse, 1949. The family of R.N. Wyse

Captivity's physical toll is evident in this postwar photo, in which Robert Wyse (right) looks, if anything, older than his father (left).
The family of R.N. Wyse

word about his wife and young son (also named Robert Nicholson Wyse) since 1941, but it was hardly a surprise that the marriage that he had run away from was irretrievably lost. He and his wife divorced, and then Wyse embarked on a long automobile tour of North America for some much needed relaxation. Upon his return to Canada, he spent some time convalescing at Portage Vale, where he met a young woman named Laura Teakles. They married in 1948, and their daughter, Ruth, was born when Wyse was fifty-one.

One of his first acts upon his release was to arrange for the retrieval of the diary that he had buried in December 1943 (in all likelihood, he contacted a Dutch prisoner or civilian he knew). The many scraps of paper eventually reached Canada in a trunk containing some other meagre belongings from his Far East excursion, and Wyse and Laura's sister, Dorothy Teakles, transcribed the notes into typescript. The original diary notes, sadly, have been lost.

Like so many other Far East P.O.W.s, Robert Wyse suffered permanent health damage as a result of his captivity. His heart weakened by his experience, he died in 1967 at the age of sixty-seven.

SEEKING

I'll wander in the forest lands,
Through trees that laugh and sway;
With ardour breast the wooded slopes
To watch the close of day.

I'll climb the lonely mountain peaks;
Search down each leafy vale;
I'll seek out treasures in the loam,
Their fresh perfume inhale.

I'll pause beside the imaged lakes;
Explore the winding streams
And loiter near the waterfall,
To ponder tranquil themes.

I'll wash away the sweat and tears-
God's handiwork undone-
Sin and deceit and lust and wars
And battles never won.

I'll beg of earthly things their faith,
For calm and truth lie there-
Prelude to love and lasting peace
-The answer to my prayer.

by

R.N.Wyse.

The family of R.N. Wyse

Acknowledgments

I am thankful that Brent Wilson and Marc Milner at the University of New Brunswick's Gregg Centre decided that I might be the right person to edit Robert Wyse's diary. Cindy Brown worked quickly and efficiently to enter the early editorial changes to the manuscript. At Goose Lane Editions, Angela Williams and Julie Scriver have been incredibly helpful throughout the publishing process. Mike Bechthold did his usual excellent work on the maps, and my son, Gordon Vance, did the photo research. Much of the hard work on this project was done by my research assistant, Dorotea Gucciardo, who transcribed Robert Wyse's own transcription with her customary efficiency and grace.

I would like to thank my old friend Dr. Charles G. Roland for sharing his unparalleled knowledge of the Far East P.O.W. experience, and the members of the very active Far East P.O.W. Community, particularly Lesley Clark and Pam Stubbs, for their willingness to respond to my queries. Dr. Chris Vinden was very kind in helping me to understand Wyse's medical condition, and Kim Solis shared her knowledge of tropical diseases. Jan Krancher, a civilian prisoner in Java, was most generous with his assistance as well.

Finally, I am very grateful to the family of Robert Wyse for allowing me to help bring this diary to the reading public; it is a remarkable document, and I think that its publication would have brought him happiness.

Selected Bibliography

Audus, Leslie J. *Spice Island Slaves: A History of Japanese Prisoner-of-War Camps in Eastern Indonesia, May 1943-August 1945*. Richmond, UK: Alma, 1996.

Castle, Colin. *Lucky Alex: The Career of Group Captain A.M. Jardine, AFC, CD, RCAF (Ret'd), Seaman and Airman*. Victoria, BC: Trafford, 2001.

Chater, Les. *Behind the Fence: Life as a POW in Japan, 1942-1945*. St. Catharines, ON: Vanwell, 2001.

Cooper, George, with Dennis Holman. *Ordeal in the Sun*. London: Robert Hale, 1963.

Cowling, Anthony. *My Life with the Samurai*. Kenthurst, Australia: Kangaroo Press, 1996.

Dunlop, E.E. *The War Diaries of Weary Dunlop, Java and the Burma-Thailand Railway, 1942-1945*. Wheathampstead, UK: Lennard, 1987.

Faulk, Stanley L., ed. *Foo: A Japanese-American Prisoner of the Rising Sun. The Secret Prison Diary of Frank "Foo" Fujita*. Denton, TX: University of North Texas Press, 1993.

Fitzgerald, Jack. *The Jack Ford Story: Newfoundland's POW in Nagasaki*. St John's, NL: Creative Book Publishing, 2007.

Fletcher-Cooke, John. *The Emperor's Guest, 1942-45*. London: Leo Cooper, 1971.

Forbes, Flight Lieutenant F.A. "Medical Report on Certain Prisoner of War Camps in Java and the Ambon Group, with Special Reference to Diseases Encountered and Treatments Thereof, April 1942–August 1945." Unpublished.

Franklin, William. *Through Adversity to Attainment*. Victoria, BC: Trafford, 2005.

Griffiths, Bill, with Hugh Popham. *Blind to Misfortune: A Story of Great Courage in the Face of Adversity.* London: Leo Cooper, 1989.

Home, James. *Their Last Tenko.* Huddersfield, UK: Quoin, 1989.

Java FEPOW 1942 Club. *Prisoners in Java: Accounts by Allied Prisoners of War in the Far East (1942-1945) Captured in Java.* Southampton, UK: Hamwic, 2007.

Jefford, Wing Commander C.G. *RAF Squadrons: A Comprehensive Record of the Movement and Equipment of all RAF Squadrons and their Antecedents since 1912.* Shrewsbury, UK: Airlife, 1988.

Krancher, Jan A., ed. *The Defining Years of the Dutch East Indies, 1942-1949: Survivors' Accounts of Japanese Invasion and Enslavement of Europeans and the Revolution that Created Free Indonesia.* Jefferson, NC: McFarland & Company, 1996.

MacCarthy, Aidan. *A Doctor's War.* Cork: Collins Press, 2005 [1979].

Peacock, Don. *The Emperor's Guest: The Diary of a British Prisoner-of-War of the Japanese in Indonesia.* Cambridge: Oleander Press, 1989.

Philps, Richard. *Prisoner Doctor: An Account of the Experiences of a Royal Air Force Medical Officer during the Japanese Occupation of Indonesia, 1942 to 1954.* Brighton, UK: The Book Guild, 1996.

Poidevin, Leslie. *Samurais and Circumcisions.* Adelaide, Australia: privately published, 1985.

Shores, Christopher, and Brian Cull, with Yasuho Izawa. *Bloody Shambles*, vol. 1, *The Drift to War to the Fall of Singapore.* London: Grub Street, 1992.

———. *Bloody Shambles*, vol. 2, *The Defence of Sumatra to the Fall of Burma.* London: Grub Street, 1996.

Stofer, Ken. *Dear Mum: The Story of Victor Edward "Candy" Syrett, a Canadian in the Royal Air Force during World War Two.* Victoria, BC: Kenlyn, 1991.

Stubbs, Les, and Pam Stubbs. *Unsung Heroes of the Royal Air Force: The Far East Prisoners of War, 1941-1945.* Grantham, UK: Barny Books, 2002.

van der Post, Laurens. *Night of the New Moon.* London: Hogarth Press, 1970.

Photo Credits

Photo on the front cover (ART26492) and on pages 72 and 73 appear courtesy of the Australian War Memorial. The photos on pages 6, 10, 11, 12, 13, 49, 58,114, 128, 129, and 130 appear courtesy of the family of R.N. Wyse. The photos on pages 19 and 21 appear courtesy of E.P. Smith. The photo on page 25 appears courtesy of www.footnote.com. The sketches on pages 37, 40, 49, 70, 83, 90, 94, and on the back cover appear courtesy of Jan Krancher. The sketch on page 56 appears courtesy of Dr. Leslie Andus. The maps on pages 13 and 15 are by Mike Bechthold. All illustrative material is reproduced by permission.

Index

The New Brunswick Military Heritage Project

The New Brunswick Military Heritage Project, a non-profit organization devoted to public awareness of the remarkable military heritage of the province, is an initiative of the Brigadier Milton F. Gregg, VC, Centre for the Study of War and Society of the University of New Brunswick. The organization consists of museum professionals, teachers, university professors, graduate students, active and retired members of the Canadian Forces, and other historians. We welcome public involvement. People who have ideas for books or information for our database can contact us through our website: www.unb.ca/nbmhp.

One of the main activities of the New Brunswick Military Heritage Project is the publication of the New Brunswick Military Heritage Series with Goose Lane Editions. This series of books is under the direction of Marc Milner, Director of the Gregg Centre, and J. Brent Wilson, Publications Director of the Gregg Centre at the University of New Brunswick. Publication of the series is supported by a grant from the Canadian War Museum.

Canadian
War Museum

Musée canadien
de la guerre

The New Brunswick Military Heritage Series

Volume 1
Saint John Fortifications, 1630-1956, Roger Sarty and Doug Knight

Volume 2
Hope Restored: The American Revolution and the Founding of New Brunswick, Robert L. Dallison

Volume 3
The Siege of Fort Beauséjour, 1755, Chris M. Hand

Volume 4
Riding into War: The Memoir of a Horse Transport Driver, 1916-1919, James Robert Johnston

Volume 5
The Road to Canada: The Grand Communications Route from Saint John to Quebec, W. E. (Gary) Campbell

Volume 6
Trimming Yankee Sails: Pirates and Privateers of New Brunswick, Faye Kert

Volume 7
War on the Home Front: The Farm Diaries of Daniel MacMillan, 1914-1927, ed. Bill Parenteau and Stephen Dutcher

About the Author

Jonathan F. Vance was educated at McMaster University, Queen's University, and York University before joining the Department of History at The University of Western Ontario in 1997. He was named the Canada Research Chair in Conflict and Culture in 2001 and in 2003; his contribution to the study of history was further recognized with a Premier's Research Excellence Award, to study the relationship between government, culture, and nationalism. His work on the First World War, aviation, national building projects, prisoners of war, and social memory crosses disciplinary boundaries to embrace history, cultural studies, communications theory, geography, and sociology. Among his books are the award-winning *Death So Noble: Memory, Meaning, and the First World War* (1997), *High Flight: Aviation and the Canadian Imagination* (2002), *Building Canada: People and Projects That Made the Nation* (2006), *The Encyclopedia of Prisoners of War and Internment* (2006), and *Unlikely Soldiers: How Two Canadians Fought the Secret War Against Nazi Occupation* (2008).